LEADERSHIP
RITES
OF
PASSAGE

*The Journey of the Aspiring Leader
and the Methods of the Mentor*

RICK TIRRELL

LEADERSHIP RITES OF PASSAGE
THE JOURNEY OF THE ASPIRING LEADER AND THE METHODS OF THE MENTOR

iUniverse books may be ordered through booksellers or by contacting:

iUniverse
1663 Liberty Drive
Bloomington, IN 47403
www.iuniverse.com
844-349-9409

Because of the dynamic nature of the Internet, any web addresses or links contained in this book may have changed since publication and may no longer be valid. The views expressed in this work are solely those of the author and do not necessarily reflect the views of the publisher, and the publisher hereby disclaims any responsibility for them.

Any people depicted in stock imagery provided by Getty Images are models, and such images are being used for illustrative purposes only. Certain stock imagery © Getty Images.

ISBN: 978-1-6632-1459-1 (sc)
ISBN: 978-1-6632-1461-4 (hc)
ISBN: 978-1-6632-1460-7 (e)

Library of Congress Control Number: 2021902091

Print information available on the last page.

iUniverse rev. date: 02/22/2021

"Some are born great, some achieve greatness, and some have greatness thrust upon them."

- William Shakespeare, *Twelfth Night*

About the Author

For nearly thirty years, Rick Tirrell, Ph.D., has helped leaders and mentors build their skills in publicly traded companies, privately held firms, nonprofits, and government organizations. His mastery of the art and science of leadership gives the aspiring leader an actionable toolbox for developing effective leadership abilities. His seminars convert leadership theory into useful and achievable steps that every leader and mentor can take. His experience comes from frontline supervisors as well as the corner office. In addition, he has founded and led two companies himself. His Ph.D. is in psychology and this is his fourth business book. Contact Rick through the website www.navigatorgroupinc.com.

Also by Rick Tirrell

Rick's most substantial previous work was his 2009 groundbreaking book, *The Wisdom of Resilience Builders: How Our Best Leaders Create the World's Most Enduring Enterprises.* It shows how great leaders use four variables to build firms that are impact-resistant growth generators. It profiles how they create powerful internal processes that support their competitive advantage at every level of the organization. It further examines their skill at generating an adaptive strategy that prepares them to deal with competitive threats and unfavorable market shifts.

Contents

Fourth Mission: Master the Psychology of Leadership

Author's Note:

A Worthy Journey

Extraordinary leaders experience a natural process of personal growth over the span of their careers. As inexperienced leaders encounter uncomfortable challenges, they may choose to ignore those challenges, but this will not make those challenges go away. Conversely, inexperienced leaders may work to build skills that enable them to overcome each challenge and move their leadership competencies upward to a higher level. Each time they progress to a new level, they open themselves up to a new and more difficult set of challenges. This creates a process of ongoing development, leadership development.

Becoming an Extraordinary Leader

Your transition toward extraordinary leadership will be a personal journey. It always is. Within this journey, this book invites you to go on four missions. They are:

> First Mission: *Take the Lead*
> Second Mission: *Create Followers*
> Third Mission: *Become a Leader of Leaders*
> Fourth Mission: *Master the Psychology of Leadership*

Each mission contains a set of tests which must be mastered to successfully complete the whole mission. This book calls these tests Rites of Passage and it examines 16 Leadership Rites of Passage.

Joe Miller and Sagen Cruz

This is a story about how an earnest man named Joe Miller gradually becomes an extraordinary leader. His steps are intended to offer you some good leadership tools. However, this book offers a second set of tools because it also unveils the masterful insights and interventions used by Joe's mentor, Sagen Cruz. So, this is a fable about both men. In fact, all the characters in this story are fictitious.

Please study the journey of Joe Miller. Gain your own insights from his successes and struggles. He will reveal his weaknesses and insecurities. You will see how he discovers ways to address each challenge, mobilize his people, and build momentum in his organization. Study Sagen as well. Watch how he sometimes allows silence to do his work for him. Watch as he skillfully touches the nerve Joe so hesitantly exposes. Observe as Sagen shares his wisdom. You can become the wise mentor that is Sagen.

This Book

This book is intended to be enjoyable and easy to read but also have some substance to it. Sagen will introduce Joe to many of the great theorists in the leadership literature. He will point to these theories and state what each one offers but he will not provide a detailed summary of them. These classical theories were developed by great thinkers; each one is a treasure. As you go through this book, I hope you will have your interest piqued and you will select a few for your own reading.

You will see Joe jump ahead and go backward as this story maneuvers through, compresses, and elongates time. Also, you will see Sagen refer Joe to books long before they are written. This technique of timeline violation will happen often and is intended to make the fable interesting and helpful.

It might be best to read just one chapter each week and contemplate your own Rites of Passage as you share Joe's life and attempt to imitate Sagen. Please know that you are on a worthy journey.

This book is designed for:

- Leadership Development Self-Study
- Mentor Skill-Building
- An Agenda for a 16 Session Leadership Seminar
- A Train the Trainer Protocol

I hope you enjoy reading this story as much as I have enjoyed writing it.

Prologue:

A Moment with Joe Miller

January third is a cold day in Chicago as all 125 employees of the Jergan Conveyor Company enter the community college lecture hall. They sit, waiting and quietly talking among themselves. There is a powerful sense of anxiety in the room. Or maybe it is just fear.

The meeting starts at 9:00, right on time. His meetings always start on time. He adjusts the microphone behind the lecturer's podium. A few seconds later, he removes it and steps away from the podium so he can better connect with his audience. He is tall and thin, in his late-40s, dressed in a sports jacket and khaki pants. The audience studies him. He maintains eye contact as he begins to speak.

"Good afternoon. My name is Joe Miller. Thank you all for coming despite this terrible weather. I am happy to meet you. I hope as we go into the future together, I will get to know each of you and you will get to know me.

"As you know, our company, KC Miller Conveyor, has purchased your firm. I am sure you are wondering how this will affect you. You must be wondering what my intentions are, and whether I am the kind of guy you will want to work for. I hope you will decide I am.

"To begin our conversation, I must say a few things about what I do not intend to do. I do not intend to have a layoff here. I do not intend to simply engage in a cost-cutting campaign and then sell this company to some investment bankers in a year or two. Let's leave that kind of stuff to the people on Wall Street.

"I can tell you what my hopes are. I hope every one of you stays with us, and I hope a year from now you will be glad you did. The

1

main reason we bought this company is because of you, its people. We think you are great people who have tremendous abilities. We think your customers are impressively loyal, but this loyalty is not because of the conveyors you build. We think your customers are loyal because they have gotten to know you and they trust you will do everything within your power to help them succeed.

"Please know I will do everything within my power to help you succeed. I must be frank with you, however. Your previous president is here in the room, and he is a good man. He and I have had many great conversations. However, he has told me that he was a good salesman but a not-so-good business owner. He also told me he was great with customers, but he was not great with operations, supply chain issues, accounting systems, and all those things.

"So, if you will stay with me, I think together we can move this business up and into its next level. We can install modern warehousing systems, manage our inventory, and improve our processes. This may sound difficult, but if we can take these steps, I promise the work you do every day will be much easier.

"I am going to make a bet on you even though your operations are losing money. As you all know, there has never been a bonus here. When we generate a profit, something your company hasn't seen in years, I will give you a piece of that profit at year end. I will show you the numbers behind that profit. I will show you other numbers as well, such as waste, percent of on-time deliveries, and cycle time (the time from order to project completion). This is going to be our business together, and we will sink or swim together.

"There is another part of the bet. I know many of you work at minimum wage and do not have a health plan. That ends today. Starting today, no one will be at minimum wage. Your new wage will depend on your years of service and what you do for us, but the days of minimum wage must come to an end. So must the days in which anyone goes without a health plan.

"Before I open this up for questions, I do have two more things to say. First, I am not trying to give you gifts here. I am just trying to be fair. I do expect a lot in return. And second, welcome to the KC Miller Conveyor family. What are your questions?"

There are no questions, just stunned silence. The audience sits still and stares at Joe Miller. He waits. No questions. No one moves.

After a prolonged silence, he thanks them again for coming and walks off stage.

Nearly a year later, on December 22nd, there is another meeting in the same lecture hall. However, instead of 125 people attending, there are 150.

Joe again opens the meeting by thanking everyone for coming despite the harsh weather. He then thanks them for a remarkable year, and says he is proud of every one of them and grateful he has come to know them.

Joe goes through some numbers. Sales have increased by 18%, an impressive number in a tough industry. Waste due to design error and incorrect order fulfillment has been reduced by an astounding 75%. Turnover among hourly workers has gone from a depressing 60% to a flat zero. Not one hourly worker has quit or been fired this year.

More impressively, the sales team has mapped the profits of their various product-categories and has started pushing the more profitable lines. Cycle time has been reduced by 10%. Profits are at $2,500 per employee, so Joe announces a bonus of $1,500 per employee.

Joe asks what questions they have for him. No one speaks. That's because a good number of them have tears in their eyes. A few are quietly crying. The silence is broken when a man stands up in the back of the room.

He says, "Good afternoon, Joe. My name is Manny Carrera. But you know my name, Joe. You make sure to stop by and visit me every time you are in town. Heck, you know my children's names. I want to say it was the best day of my life when you bought this company. One year ago, you asked us to follow you. Joe, I think I speak for all of us when I say that I would follow you to the gates of Hell and back home again."

There is some quiet laughter in the room at Manny's overstatement, but now it is Joe whose eyes well up.

On the plane ride home, Joe revels in this good moment. As he savors it, he reminds himself that this is the easy part. He has met some basic needs of these good people, and they have responded. He has built some two-way trust. However, as he heads into the future, he knows their needs will become more sophisticated and more opaque. He wonders if he will still be able to meet those needs or even know what they are.

As he crosses the sky at 500 miles per hour, he recalls the day he first met Sagen Cruz, his leadership mentor. It was twenty-two years ago, when Joe was very eager and very green.

Case Study:

1. Here we see 47-year-old Joe Miller, who is an extraordinary leader. What leadership competencies does he display?

2. Would Joe give himself the title of extraordinary leader? Would he say he has crossed the finish line regarding his own leadership development? Can you see some developmental leadership work he still might do?

3. His company has just purchased the Jergan Conveyor Company in Chicago and the employees are fearful. What could be the sources of their fear?

4. Joe gives them many assurances, like telling them he does not intend to sell their company. To what extent do these words actually offer assurance?

5. His statement that he will get to know each of them and they will get to know him suggests a very personal type of leadership. Is this a competent approach? What can go wrong with this approach? Are there other approaches which could be equally competent?

6. Are his criticisms of the previous president simply insults or is this the beginning of having open and honest dialogue? Is he displaying trust here by engaging in respectful conflict? Were his words about the previous president a surprise to the employees?

7. Was this group's amazingly successful performance during the year simply the result of Joe's speech? If not, what might have motivated the employees to do so well?

First Mission: Take the Lead

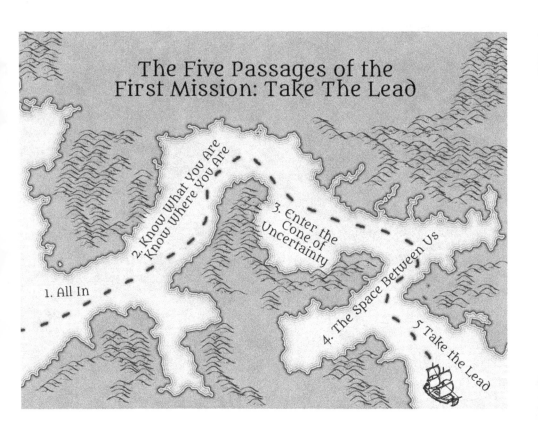

The Five Passages of the
First Mission: Take The Lead

2. Know What You Are
Know Where You Are

3. Enter the
Cone of
Uncertainty

4. The Space Between Us

1. All In

5 Take the Lead

Chapter One

First Rite of Passage: All In

This story, in fact, begins two decades earlier, as young Joe Miller motors up a long steep driveway toward what appears to be a massive log cabin. His rental car is rear-wheel drive, and the back tires slip a few times on the loose gravel. He has never been to Colorado before and is awestruck by the mountain view and fresh air.

As he walks up the front steps, he realizes this is no log cabin. It looks more like a resort clubhouse. He knocks and waits. The door opens slowly, and a man appears. Joe is surprised by the man's aged appearance and thinks he looks a little like Albert Einstein. The man has a slight accent, but Joe can't discern what it is.

"Welcome, Joe. Please call me Sagen and please come in. Would you like something to eat or drink?"

"Oh, no thank you," says Joe as his eyes wander around the massive room and fixate on the fireplace. There are so many windows on the walls, it feels as if he is still outside.

Sagen says, "I see you are as impressed with this place as I am. It was a hunting lodge at one time, and that fireplace was designed so hunters could stand inside it next to the fire while the ice on their beards and clothes melted. That's why it's so big."

Sagen invites Joe to sit and motions in the general direction of a soft leather couch and chair. Sagen's chair obviously is the one that swivels.

"I hear you know my grandson David," says Sagen.

"Yes," says Joe. "We served together in Iraq, and we both got out a year and a half ago. We are great friends. He told me you give advice to businesses. Is that right?"

"Well, Joe, I mostly stay here in the mountains and they each pay me handsomely every month to think about their companies and to answer their questions. I am only face-to-face with them about 10 hours a month."

Joe asks, "David told me you worked with the space program?"

"Yes, Joe. I worked with the SPOKES Space Probe Program nearly 30 years ago. This was among the first international cooperative space programs."

Joe asks, "SPOKES?"

Sagen replies, "Most people don't understand where the name SPOKES comes from. Imagine a ball that has spokes coming out in all directions. Now imagine the ball is the planet Earth. We tend to think of our solar system as being at the center of the universe, but it isn't. It's just one part of an endless array of galaxies. The plan was to send out probes in all directions to the edges of the known universe. These probes would conduct scientific studies in space, including the planets they would encounter along the way. Probes are unmanned spacecraft and the experiments would be done by robots inside the probes. The applications of their discoveries could be immense for industry, agriculture, and medicine."

"May I ask how you fit in with this program, Sagen?"

"This all began in the 1990s and involved scientists from six nations. Unfortunately, each country and each department worked quite independently, like separate fiefdoms. They tracked their progress during the first two years and, based on their rate of productivity, they calculated it would take 40 years before they could launch their first series of probes. Of course, this slow pace was unacceptable so they asked me to help them work faster. I told them

I could not simply get them to work faster. Instead, I offered to help them to work smarter. I gave them what they needed, not what they asked for.

"I created a new organizational chart for all participants and called it a matrix organization. On the *x*-axis I listed every department and subdepartment. I did the same on the *y*- axis. Then I looked to see who was whose internal customer. On a second chart I created the same *x*-and *y*-axes and connected tasks across departments. Those became cross-functional teams. Engineers, manufacturers and designers from multiple countries all worked on the same teams at the same time. One person might get direction and receive performance reviews from supervisors in three or four different departments. Using this new structure allowed them to launch their first sequence of rockets in only seven years. Pretty good, wouldn't you say?"

"So, you invented the matrix org chart as well as cross-functional teams?" Joe asks.

"Yes, simply as a way to create more efficient work processes." [1]

"I might be in the wrong place," Joe says. "I'm not the space program or any of the big corporations you have worked with and I am sure I cannot afford you."

Sagen says, "I don't think you are in the wrong place, Joe. Not from what David has told me. Why don't we begin in the beginning? Please tell me about yourself."

"I came back from the war to work in my father's company a year and a half ago. He was the founder of KC Miller Conveyor. The name really speaks to Kansas City, that's the KC; and Miller, that's our family name. Hence, KC Miller Conveyor. We build and install conveyor systems for everyone from small mom and pop warehouse operations to big car manufacturers. We are a small company, really."

Sagen says, "Sounds like a good business."

Joe says, "The problem is, after I worked for my father for six months, he died of a heart attack. The business continued to do very well after that, so last summer I borrowed four million dollars to buy another conveyor company in Des Moines. This was our first acquisition and I was scared to death to borrow such a huge amount of money. Again, things went well until the events of six months ago. As you know, that's when the economy fell into a deep recession. Business dropped off and new orders came to a complete stop. Of the small number of projects we are working on now, over 80% of our customers are on progress payment plans. This means we are requiring them to pay us as we complete each phase of the job. We've never had to use progress payments before. I am the 25-year-old president and owner of this company, and I know I am young and inexperienced. I have 75 employees who rely on me. The worst part of all this is that I have a deep sense of dread that I am not capable of fixing this. Maybe I'm not the right man for the job."

Sagen says, "But Joe, I asked you to tell me about yourself. You are telling me about your business. Please?"

As Sagen turns his chair to face the windows, he listens.

"Okay. Well, I am an only child," Joe says. "I was a good boy, always trying to please, and my parents didn't need to discipline me much. I was in a variety of sports but didn't really like contact sports. When I was a sophomore in high school, the cross-country track coach approached me. He asked me to come to a practice, where I found that I was just as comfortable running as walking. I was competitive, though. I would get to the front and if someone tried to pass me, I would just speed up. I hated to have anyone get ahead of me. This meant that sometimes in the middle of a long-distance run I would sprint. I just had to win.

"I played trumpet in the high school band. I loved the music, but I loved the great fellowship in the band even more. If you know anything about it, the brass section often carries the melody for the entire orchestra, so we all had to perform well. We became close because we each needed the others to perform well. Often an older student would tutor a younger one. I am still in touch with most of them.

"My parents did well financially and this allowed me to get a pilot's license while I was in high school. I stopped flying when I went to college, where I got a degree in mechanical engineering.

"While I was in college, 9-11 happened. I can still remember watching TV as the Twin Towers fell. That deeply affected me. Two days later I learned that the son of one of my mother's sorority sisters had died in the attack. I had only met my mother's friend a couple of times when she had come to town, but I liked her. This brought the whole thing to life for me. This was happening to real people. All this inspired me to enroll in ROTC. Of course, this meant that upon graduation I was going to be a lieutenant in the army.

"When the army reviewed my records, they gave me a chance to decide whether to be an army engineer or to use my pilot's license. They left the decision up to me, but I knew they really needed pilots so I chose to fly. I was sent to Fort Rucker in Alabama where I became a helicopter pilot. I think my trainers could see I was a gentle soul. They knew I would've made a terrible attack helicopter pilot but would be good at rescue. So, eventually they sent me to a combat zone as a medevac helicopter pilot."

Sagen interrupts, "A medevac pilot?"

"Yes, I got there just in time for the Battle of Karbala. I flew into areas where there were wounded troops and evacuated them. It sounds more daring than it was. I liked being a helper. I also liked the fellowship I found in the army."

Sagen says, "That's where you met David."

"Yes, I flew him out."

"David says you did more than that."

Joe replies, "In medical evacuation, we had a thing called 'The Golden Hour'. This means we greatly increased the seriously wounded soldier's chance of survival if we could get him to the appropriate level of care in one hour or less. I picked up David first, and then I got called to another casualty. The second guy had severe trauma, and because I had a good medic on board, I flew them both right past our battalion aid and took them to the trauma center at Joint Base Balad in Baghdad. This took much more than an hour and I knew my commander would chew me out, but it saved that second guy's life."

Sagen asks, "And it got David to a higher level of care?"

"Yes. David was just lucky I got the second dispatch."

Sagen replies, "David says he was just lucky to meet you."

Joe remains quiet for a moment.

Sagen asks, "So what is your question for me, Joe?"

"What should I do?" asks Joe. "This recession is killing us. New bids are non-existent. I need to pay my people, and I need to make payments on a four-million-dollar debt."

Sagen gives some concrete advice, "Joe, in a time like this, you should start by executing the basics. Reduce fixed expenses, restructure your debt in order to shore up your free cash flow, cut as many variable expenses as you can, and figure out which product lines are most and least profitable. Those are the basic steps to take during a sudden downturn."

As Sagen speaks, Joe takes careful notes. Sagen says, "I know a man who would be willing to lend you the money you need for that four-million-dollar debt. He will spread the payments out in a very comfortable manner for you. I will call him."

Sagen continues, "As I said, Joe, those are the basics. However, there is one issue here that is of greater importance. I must ask you Joe, are you *All In*?"

"*All In*? What does *All In* mean?" Joe asks.

"Have you invested your whole self into this business? What were you trying to do with it before the recession began? Is the business built to sell or built to last? Would you be willing to die trying to save it as you were willing to die trying to save your troops? There are many people who call themselves leaders but are not *All In*. It really is nothing more than a job for them. You must decide whether you are *All In*. Please don't answer me now, Joe. We can talk about it next week."

Joe says, "I am just trying to save my business, but I'm not sure how much more of myself I can give. Are there some steps you can recommend I take on all of this?"

"Okay, Joe. This is a little like the SPOKES problem. You are asking for one thing, to help save your business, and I will give you something else. However, what I give you will solve your problem. I will start you on the journey toward becoming an extraordinary leader. You must understand, becoming an extraordinary leader does not happen in a single moment, nor as a result of one life-changing event. It is a process that takes a lifetime. I will send you on four missions. Each mission will contain multiple passages. I can guide you through those passages, but the work will be yours, not mine.

"Imagine you are piloting an old-fashioned ship with great sails in extremely turbulent waters. Think of each passage as a rock-filled narrow entry into a channel which leads to calmer waters. Successfully navigating your way through this passage and into the nearby open waters will make you a better leader. However, soon the seas will become rough again, and another passage will call to you. You will either succeed or fail to traverse each passage. If you fail, each passage will continue to call to you until you successfully master it. Ignoring a piece of this work will not make it go away. These passages do not need to be done sequentially, although some do tend to present themselves earlier than others.

"Always be aware, Joe, there are four missions and each mission has multiple passages within it. I believe these passages are so important that I have begun to call the process of mastering them, Rites of Passage. You are already on your first mission. It is called *Take the Lead.* Your first Rite of Passage within this mission is called *All In.*"

Sagen continues, "Please remember, Joe, this is a journey. It is a journey of tests, and gaining the competencies needed to master each new challenge will move your development further toward becoming an extraordinary leader. Do you want to become an extraordinary leader, Joe?"

Joe says, "I am trying to become the best leader humanly possible. If that's an extraordinary leader, then that's what I want to be."

Sagen sets an agenda, "Joe, I have a good sense of where our work should begin. You have a few choices about what competitive strategy you might want to engage at this point. Also, I think we should talk about what stage of development your firm is in now. If you can become clear on these two topics, it will help you greatly as you strengthen your leadership and build your team. It will help you to become *All In*."

Joe is scribbling notes as he says, "Okay, my competitive strategy and my firm's stage of development."

Sagen asks, "Will you please come back next week? And between now and then, read *The Wisdom of Resilience Builders*. [2] It will give you a framework to address these two important issues."

Joe says, "Okay, but I can't pay you. I certainly can't pay you what you normally get."

Sagen replies, "Tell you what, Joe. Let's do it this way. You come here once a week for a while, then less frequently. You pay me nothing for now. When you are able to pay, you should decide how much my advice has been worth and pay me that amount."

Joe smiles, shakes the hand of his new mentor, and heads out to buy a book.

Joe's Rite of Passage:

1. Wisely, Joe seeks a mentor.
2. Joe reveals he is afraid that he does not have the competence to turn this business around.
3. Joe shows that he cares about his people, and that he feels the weight of the enterprise on his own shoulders.
4. Joe is receptive to the idea that he must be *All In*. However, he needs time to understand how this really applies to him.
5. Joe hears Sagen explain the concept of "Rites of Passage". These are predictable stages in his formation as an extraordinary leader. Each involves tasks he must master so he can proceed to the next stage.
6. Joe accepts the idea that each passage will remain in place, waiting for him to do the work it calls him to do. This work will not go away simply because he ignores it.
7. Joe shakes the hand of his new mentor. This displays the beginning of a working relationship.

Sagen's Mentoring Process:

1. Sagen welcomes Joe warmly.

2. He gives a very brief description of himself to establish credibility. After that, he will never again reveal anything personal about himself. The focus is only on Joe.

3. At the mentor's request, "Please tell me about yourself," new mentees always give an answer that describes the workplace, so Sagen asks the question again.

4. Sagen listens for Joe's interpersonal style (he likes fellowship, and he bonded well with the folks in the band and the army), intellectual ability (he got a pilot's license as a teenager and majored in mechanical engineering), temperament (Joe describes himself as a gentle soul and a rescuer), and level of ambition (He could have sold the business when his father died but chose to run it himself. Recently, he borrowed a large amount of money to expand.).

5. He sees that when Joe was a medevac pilot, he was quite able to derive a plan even if it involved risk and was outside the established protocol. He also sees that Joe was able to execute the plan quickly and competently (flying past battalion aid to a trauma center). However, Sagen sees that in his current situation Joe is frozen in place.

6. Sagen observes that he has given Joe an opportunity to self-aggrandize (to brag about himself in recalling the moments he saved David and the other soldier) but Joe doesn't do so. Rather, Joe remains humble and tells a story of just trying to do the right thing.

7. Sagen notes that Joe does not enter the process requesting to improve his leadership skills. He wants a concrete solution to a very real problem.

8. Sagen offers something to solve the problem in a tangible way; a man who will lend. The mentor can help in this concrete manner when appropriate, early in the mentoring process, but just once. He should not do the mentee's work for him or her.

9. Sagen gives Joe a reading assignment. This engages Joe in the process. Whether or not Joe does the reading assignment will inform Sagen of Joe's level of commitment.

10. Sagen ends the session by asking two probing questions: "Are you *All In*?" and "Are you trying to become an extraordinary leader?"

Sagen's Mentoring Process:

11.   Sagen knows Joe has much work to do, and some of this work will make Joe struggle. He sees that Joe is a nice guy, and perhaps lacking assertiveness in his leadership. He observes that Joe wishes to continue his father's way of doing business. He believes that because Joe is a rescuer, he is likely to try to solve company problems all by himself. This notion of Joe's independence is further supported by the fact that he was a cross country runner, which is a solo sport. He was a medevac pilot, as well. There was often just one pilot on those helicopters, so Joe will want to steer the company single-handedly.

12.   Sagen does not offer any of these insights to Joe at this early stage. He knows these insights will unfold when Joe becomes ready to address them.

13.   In shaking Joe's hand, Sagen commits to his role as mentor.

Case Study:

1. Sagen describes this as a journey of tests. Do you agree that becoming an extraordinary leader involves a journey of tests? What are the most common tests anyone might face on this journey?

2. Sagen tells Joe if he fails or ignores any one of the tests it will remain there until he masters it. Do you agree this is how the process works? Please give some examples.

3. Is it necessary for you to work with a mentor to become an extraordinary leader? Could you just do this work without help? What about simply imitating someone you regard to be an extraordinary leader?

4. Sagen will avoid speaking about himself. Why? Is good mentoring always a one-directional conversation?

5. Joe describes himself as having been a good boy and eager to please. Assume his self-description is accurate. What problems might he encounter on his journey as a result of these traits?

6. What if this were a story not about a good boy, but rather about a man who had been rebellious as a teen and still carried a mild rebellious trait as an adult? What problems might this man encounter?

7. Is it necessary for the leader to be *All In*? What about work-family balance?

8. In order to become an extraordinary leader, is it necessary for the person to be consciously aware that this journey of leadership development is his/her life's work?

Chapter Two

Second Rite of Passage: Know What You Are, Know Where You Are

One week later, as Joe steps onto Sagen's porch, the door opens and Sagen greets him warmly. Joe enters, takes the same seat as last time, opens his pad of paper, and prepares to take notes.

After some small talk, Joe offers, "I have an answer to your question. I am *All In*. I am willing to do anything that is legal and ethical to make this company survive. If this means I must work night and day, weekends, and holidays, then I will do it. If it means I will sometimes sleep at the office and never take a vacation, then so be it. If this requires me to invest my own money until I go bankrupt personally, then that's how it will be."

Joe continues, "When you asked me last week if this was similar to my medevac missions, I needed time to think about your question. Now, I know it is much the same. People's lives are depending on me. It's not just that, though. It is also about the fact that I hate to lose. I will not let this business fail."

"Very good, Joe," Sagen says. "Very good."

Sagen waits for a moment. He continues, "Joe, please recall that in our last meeting I said you will go on four missions. Your first mission is *Take the Lead.* By this I mean you must be the leader. Don the garb of a leader. Walk, talk, and think like a leader. Own it. Make it part of your identity. Your first Rite of Passage in this mission is called *All In.* I am glad you have decided to be *All In.* Now we must look at your second Rite of Passage within this mission."

Joe says, "I understand."

Sagen asks, "In a military operation, what are the two most important questions a leader must be able to answer at all times?"

Joe replies, "You have to know what you are and where you are."

Sagen asks, "Ah, so you were a medevac helicopter pilot, yes?"

"Yes."

"Did you have guns or gunners on board?"

"No."

"So, you would not engage the enemy in battle? You would rescue and evade. Correct?"

"Yes."

Sagen asks, "You knew what to do because you knew what you were and what you weren't."

Sagen pushes on, "The book, *Resilience Builders*, suggests a durable company can be built on one of four competitive platforms. Which one relates most closely to your business?"

Joe asks for a moment to jot down some thoughts. He makes a small chart:

Efficient Platform firms build tremendous internal and external efficiencies to reduce waste and lower costs. They pass those savings on to the consumer. Most big-box discount stores and Internet retailers are built on Efficient Platform.

Creative Platform firms invent and create new products. Inventing and developing products is extremely costly so they take a lot of risk. Pharmaceutical companies are Creative Platform firms.

Marketing Platform firms advertise, but they do much more than that. They divide their market into segments and attempt to meet the specific needs of those segments. Brand image is well crafted and extremely important. Car companies are built on the Marketing Platform.

Relationship Platform firms' primary motive is to increase the attachment a customer has with them. They do the customer favors, even if this means they lose money doing so. They get to know their customers well and use that knowledge to do something pleasing for them. Many architecture firms are built on Relationship Platform.

"My father began growing this business twenty-seven years ago by building deep relationships based on trust and high service. He didn't care, and neither do I, if the company would lose money by doing someone a favor. For example, if the owner of a small factory were to call at 8 o'clock on a Friday evening and say his conveyor is down because it needed a $12.00 motor coupling, my father would go to the warehouse, get the coupling, and deliver it personally. This is terribly inefficient for us, but we believe this kind of service shows our customers that we understand what their lives are like and that we know what their needs are. We believe that by our showing this, the customer becomes attached to us. Every favor we do increases this attachment. None of our competitors operate this way."

Sagen asks, "What about your firm's relationship with employees?"

Joe replies, "They are like family. We go out of our way to show them we care. And just as we seek opportunities to do a customer a favor, we try to do the same with our employees."

Sagen says, "So it is true indeed, you are a Relationship Platform company."

Joe nods.

Sagen continues, "I am convinced you know what you are. Now please describe for me where you are."

Joe appears to be quietly thoughtful for a moment. He says, "After reading the book, I believe we are a temporarily injured steady-state company. This means we have had a steady stream of orders for nearly three decades and that everyone in the firm expects this to continue for a very long time. But we are temporarily injured at this moment. Our Relationship Platform strategy has worked well for us. We have loyal customers and have generated prosperity for everyone who works for us. We would be very stable except for this economic recession."

Sagen turns slowly in his chair and gazes out the windows. He is quiet. After some time, he turns back toward Joe and says, "Please allow me to challenge your thinking just a little. You believe your problems are all due to the recession, which has been ongoing for about six months. However, although this recession is a severe one, we will likely climb out of it as interest rates continue to be reduced. I am convinced your problems are greater than just the recession. You have said you recently bought a competitor. May I ask how this competitor was doing prior to the acquisition?"

Joe responds, "They were struggling financially."

Sagen says, "I have been studying your industry, and I believe it is undergoing a strategic shift. You are correct in that your Relationship Platform has somewhat insulated you from this shift, but did your financial problems start suddenly, or did they develop gradually?"

Joe responds, "We have been having some difficulty, losing bids against our competitors, especially for large manufacturers, like the car companies. We figured they were just undercutting our price."

"Joe, you have told me your customer-base is everything from mom-and-pop shops to large automobile companies. You must consider what is occurring in your industry. It seems to me, the conveyor space is splitting into two levels, small shops, and big players. You have decided not to choose either of these new pathways. This suggests you will become what we call, 'stuck in the middle', neither small nor big. You run the risk of losing your market entirely. I have observed that the one difference between small and big players in your industry is whether or not they use LEAN manufacturing methods. Have you heard of this?"

"Yes," Joe replies. "However, I must be honest; I haven't paid much attention to LEAN. As you know, it's quite new."

"It is new here, Joe, but it has been going on in Japan for several years. It began in the Japanese auto industry, and now the American auto industry is replicating these methods. So are most other manufacturers. This is the basis of the restructuring of your conveyor industry. Manufacturers would want you to compress the processes you use to build conveyors, install them overnight, and custom-fit them to their unique needs. They will want you to know which parts need to be replaced before they are due and to have those parts, and only those parts, available at the right moment. All of this is intended to increase speed and eliminate waste. Joe, your industry is in the midst of a revolution and you seem not to know it."

Joe is listening.

Sagen continues, "Do you accept that your market is changing as I have described?"

"Yes. I see that. We have talked about it, but we don't see it coming very soon."

"Sooner than you think, Joe. It has begun already."

Sagen says, "I believe your firm is in the early stages of what *Resilience Builders* calls 'degeneration'. By this, I mean it is in the process of a permanent decline if you do not change strategy. Please consider the possibility that over the years, your organization may have become complacent, too comfortable. Perhaps your father saw his primary role as being a good caretaker of his employees and they were glad to be taken care of. This complacency is almost always followed by degeneration. Also, a great many conveyor companies across the country have been in degeneration. That's why the business in Des Moines was up for sale."

"What would I expect to see internally if we are in a state of degeneration?" asks Joe.

Sagen asks, "May I ask whether there have been internal stresses in your organization?"

"Yes, there have been some strange occurrences. First, I have heard rumors that the employees are saying this company isn't as good as it used to be and they blame me. They are very unhappy. Second, John Fisher, our vice president of sales barged into my office and said that this is a sinking ship and, because I am president, I should have seen it coming. He said our poor performance is all my fault. To my great surprise, he quit on the spot. I have not been sure what to make of these events. I am upset and puzzled. Clearly, there are things going on that make no sense to me."

Sagen speaks, "Nasty rumors and outbursts like John's often occur in an organization that is in a state of degeneration. The employees blame you, even for things that are not your fault. You did not create this recession. This is a challenge within your first leadership mission, *Take the Lead*. This Rite of Passage is called, *Know What You Are, Know Where You Are.*"

Sagen continues, "You have described *what* you are quite accurately. You are a Relationship Platform company. I have challenged you to view *where* you are a little differently from how you see it. If you accept you are in degeneration, then can you begin to accept that your employees are just looking for someone to blame, whether it makes sense to do so or not? Can this help you to avoid taking their criticisms too personally? This would be a great step forward on your journey toward becoming an extraordinary leader."

"I can work on it," Joe answers. "But it won't be easy."

Sagen consults, "Let's go back to talking about your competitive platform for a moment, please. Let's review *what* you are again. We both see that your firm is clearly built on the Relationship Platform. However, if your customers are poised to require more and more efficiencies, shouldn't you consider shifting your competitive platform to Efficient Platform? Wouldn't this offer you greater ability to meet their needs for speed and accuracy?"

Joe replies with a sense of urgency, "But we are a Relationship Platform company. It's in our DNA. It's the way we walk and the way we talk. It is how we relate to the world. Even if I would try to change to another competitive platform, I don't see how I could convince my people to change. And I'm not sure they could learn the entire collection of skills which would be needed to support a different platform. My plan all along here has been that when the recession ends, we will need to go around and strengthen our relationships with our customers. This means we would just dial up our Relationship Platform once again. You are suggesting this will not be enough."

Sagen allows a few moments of silence while Joe regains his composure. He speaks, "Joe, you are already traveling on your journey toward becoming an extraordinary leader. I have suggested the Rite of Passage that is calling you now is *Know What You Are, Know Where You Are*. I believe your view of what and where you are is based more on the past than the present. Your competitive environment has changed and this is calling you to change what you are. Regarding where you are, your company has likely become too comfortable and this is calling you to acknowledge that your firm is in degeneration. You should give this Rite of Passage some thought."

Joe says, "I don't know how to explain this to people. I don't really know how to frame up the problem, and I don't have a solution to offer them. This is all so ambiguous. What should I do next?"

Sagen responds in a reassuring tone, "Joe, you believe it is up to you alone to provide a solution to this problem. However, at this moment you do not see a solution. Your revenues are declining, and I have just suggested they will continue to decline. The next thing for us to do together is to decide how to address this uncertainty. Joe, will I see you in one week?"

Joe's Rite of Passage:

1. Joe announces to Sagen that he is *All In*. This is an important turning point that signifies that he is a true leader and not just an extension of his father's legacy. It is his firm now.
2. Joe correctly states that his firm is built on the Relationship Platform. Embracing this platform will influence how he leads. This is "*what*" his firm is.
3. Joe and Sagen disagree about "*where*" Joe's firm is. Joe believes it is a comfortable steady-state firm which is temporarily injured.
4. Joe resists the notion that there has been a permanent change in his competitive environment. He resists the idea of altering his Relationship Platform.
5. Because Joe does not believe his company is in degeneration, he cannot use the concept of degeneration to explain some employees' hostility toward him, such as that shown in the angry resignation of his sales manager.
6. Joe believes it is up to him to find the solution to the current problems, as we see from his comment, "I don't know how to explain this to people. I don't really know how to frame up the problem, and I don't have a solution to offer them."

Sagen's Mentoring Process:

1. When Joe says, "I'm *All In*," Sagen gives him confirmation. "Very good, Joe. Very good."
2. Sagen connects Joe's pledge to be *All In* with this mission, "You must *Take the Lead*."
3. Sagen begins to ask Adaptive Leadership questions like, "What are you?", and "Where are you?" We will learn more about Adaptive Leadership as we move through Joe's story.
4. Joe will be required to lead differently, depending on his answers to questions about what and where his company is, and whether he is *All In*.
5. Sagen instructs Joe regarding the strategic shift happening in his industry. If there is a shift occurring, this crisis will not be brief.
6. At a key moment Sagen remains silent rather than responding.
7. Sagen offers Joe the concept of uncertainty but doesn't do much with it other than simply introduce it.
8. He is patient with Joe's resistance to some of his concepts. He knows if these concepts are accurate, time will validate them.

Case Study:

1. Either the discussion facilitator or a volunteer should describe the four competitive platforms from the book, *The Wisdom of Resilience Builders*.
2. What are the defining characteristics of the four competitive platforms?
3. Can you list some companies which have established well-defined competitive platforms and have created a strong culture which supports the platform?
4. How would any leader lead his or her organization differently if he or she were in each of the four competitive platforms? Aren't leadership competencies universal, and so the platform wouldn't matter?
5. Joe cannot envision how his firm would be able to change its competitive platform. Is this a difficult thing to do? What would his new platform look like?
6. If KC Miller Conveyor were to change its competitive platform, what leadership problems might Joe encounter? Is it likely some people who excel at his current platform might do poorly in the new platform? Would he lose some people? What would be his most important leadership tasks as this occurs?
7. Either the discussion facilitator or a volunteer should describe the Developmental Frame from the book, *The Wisdom of Resilience Builders*.
8. Joe and Sagen disagree about the company's location in the Developmental Frame. Joe sees it as a temporarily injured steady-state firm. Sagen says it is in a state of degeneration in the midst of a drastically changing industry. What do you think?
9. John Fisher, Vice President of Sales, has resigned after accusing Joe of incompetency. Is this type of outburst actually typical of a company in a state of degeneration? What leadership challenges coincide with this stage in the Developmental Frame?

Chapter Three

Third Rite of Passage: Enter the Cone of Uncertainty

One week later, Joe sits in front of Sagen and says, "I almost canceled today. I have not made any progress on the issues we spoke about last week."

Sagen replies, "Everyone that comes to see me is between chapters in their lives. It is during those moments when we do not know what to do that we need the most help. I am glad you did not cancel. We have much work to do."

Joe says, "We are barely surviving, even with the loan your friend provided. It seems as if America has come to a stop. We were considering a layoff for the first time in our history, but nine more people have resigned. I don't know where they are going to go for another job in this bad economy. I think they just wanted to get away from me."

Sagen suggests, "Joe, you seem to be taking this very personally."

Joe says, "I know you say I shouldn't take it personally, Sagen, but it is personal. I can't think of anything more personal."

"When you were flying the medevac helicopter under fire, did you get upset?" Sagen asks.

Joe replies, "That was different."

"How so?"

"I was able to be outside myself. It was as if I were in a play or a movie. I had no emotions. My job was to get our guys out of there. Nothing else."

Sagen says, "This sounds a little like what we call 'going third person'."

"Going third person?"

"Yes. It is similar what you just described, but not quite so extreme. You see, in your current business situation you are personally invested in creating success for the company, and never allowing one single employee to suffer. Because of this personal investment, you are emotionally charged, and this is preventing you from looking at the situation objectively."

Joe asks, "So, I should try to look at the situation objectively?"

Sagen replies, "Yes. We call that going third person because you should pretend you are not yourself, and that you are not emotionally engaged. For a moment, you should be a third person, like a scientist objectively looking through a microscope or a doctor calmly examining an x-ray. Going third person also allows you to step back and look at the entire picture, rather than being completely immersed in one small part of what is going on. Perhaps you should ask yourself what I, Sagen, would do if I could take your place for the next year. I would not be as emotionally involved as you are. My father didn't start this company, and I don't have the same attachment to the employees that you do. I would be far more objective." [3]

Joe says, "In the military they call this being 3,000 feet above the battlefield, like a commander who can look down and see everything that's going on, although a foot soldier cannot."

"Exactly," Sagen agrees.

Joe scribbles notes on his pad and Sagen gives him some time.

Sagen says, "I have another book for you to read. It is *The Practice of Adaptive Leadership*, written by Ron Heifetz, Alexander Grashow, and Marty Linsky. [4] This book has great credibility and I will be referring to it many times as we work together."

Sagen continues, "*The Practice of Adaptive Leadership* divides the concept of leadership into two categories, Technical Leadership and Adaptive Leadership. Technical Leadership consists of accomplishing tasks your organization already knows how to do. This might include instructing your salespeople to sell more of a particular item or asking finance to get all bills out by the fifth of the month. Of course, the people in sales and finance might think these are big challenges, but these are tasks they already know how to do.

"Adaptive Leadership requires your organization to do something it doesn't really know how to do. Most often, this involves adjusting to a shift in your markets, altering your culture, or changing strategy. Adaptive Leadership is required in the moments when neither you nor your managers can see a clear pathway ahead, and it always requires the efforts of your entire team, not just you."

"Well, I surely am at a point where the pathway forward is unclear," Joe says.

Sagen persists, "Of course, this process creates great distress. This work tends to bring out conflict and perhaps the dark side of the subordinate leaders and managers under you. The stakes are great, and anxiety is high because there is no clear plan."

Joe replies, "I see what you are saying, but I still believe things will improve greatly as soon as the recession ends. We had a good business going, and we were a great team."

Sagen perseveres, "Please allow me to persist. There is a process here that could help you deal with this. As you and your team approach a complex problem that seems to have no clear answer, you all will feel anxious. It will be difficult to define what the real problem is. Equally difficult is the task of coming to consensus about which variables are in play. You all will propose different ideas and suggestions about what those variables could be, and the group will propose a wide range of solutions."

Sagen says, "It will seem as if these ideas are swirling around in a large circle, like a circular current of water. We call this the *Cone of Uncertainty*. Some good research as well as my own experiences indicate that if you will allow yourself and your team to *Enter the*

Cone of Uncertainty for enough time, and if you continue to keep the problem-solving discussions going, you will see that the problem begins to define itself more clearly. The most important variables will begin to come forward. It is as if the circular current of water is getting smaller and smaller. The Heifetz, Grashow, and Linsky book does a beautiful job of explaining this process."

Joe speaks, "Well, I understand what you're saying but I am a little uncomfortable with this. It seems you are encouraging me to tell my people I don't know what to do. That doesn't sound like good leadership to me."

"I am not suggesting you tell them you don't know what to do," Sagen responds. "I am suggesting you tell them there are multiple variables in play here and that you all, together, need to make some choices regarding each of these variables. The choices you all make on each variable will greatly influence the firm's future, so there are multiple futures that lie ahead of you at this moment."

Joe asks, "Multiple futures?"

Sagen says, "If it would make you more comfortable with the process, perhaps you could tell them you have some clear ideas and strong opinions about which choices the firm should make, but you only see the firm through your own two eyes and not through the eyes of Marketing, Sales, Design, or Production. They each will have their own eyes and perceptions. You refuse to rely on your own opinions, alone. You want to hear everything they will say, and you want the benefit of their experience before any decision is made.

"Joe, I am not proposing you display a lack self-confidence here. I think you should address this with great personal confidence as you tell them you need their expertise and their problem-solving skills so you all can engage in critical thinking and approach these important decisions. Communicate to them that you do know what to do, and that is for you to intentionally pull them into this decision-making process. Tell them that's what you know is needed now and tell them this confidently."

Joe says, "Okay, we have three new concepts going on here."

Sagen says, "Yes, all three of the concepts I am presenting to you today are connected to one another. When would it be necessary for you to go third person? Of course, the answer is when there is no clear pathway ahead. When would you find yourself being required to exercise Adaptive Leadership? When there is no clear pathway ahead. When would you need to *Enter the Cone of Uncertainty*? Again, this occurs when there is no clear pathway."

Sagen suggests, "Joe, if you can understand that Adaptive Leadership is needed at this moment, that you must become more objective by going third person, and that you must allow yourself and your leadership group to *Enter the Cone of Uncertainty* for a while, these will be your greatest steps toward becoming an extraordinary leader."

Joe sits in silence and stares at Sagen for a long moment. Joe gets up and walks over to a large window and looks outside. He remains quiet.

Joe says, "Sagen, I know that I am still on my first mission, *Take the Lead*. Also, it has become clear to me that the Rite of Passage within that mission for me now is to *Enter the Cone of Uncertainty*. This uncertainty is at the heart of the matter and it creates the need for Adaptive Leadership as well as going third person. You have given me a lot to digest here. Would it be okay if we were to postpone our next meeting for a few weeks so I can have a chance to let all this sink in?"

Joe's Rite of Passage:

1. Joe must develop the ability to go third person. He needs to observe the facts objectively, like a doctor who calmly examines an x-ray.
2. Joe should become skilled at Adaptive Leadership. Adaptive Leadership is required when he and his organization must address a circumstance which goes beyond current competencies. It will require him to look at the situation in a new way and it will require his team to develop new skills.
3. He must become comfortable allowing his team to *Enter the Cone of Uncertainty*, even when he does not know what the final outcome of this team process will be.

Sagen's Mentoring Process:

1. As the session begins, Sagen knows he is going to hit Joe with a lot of material. He does so because he believes the three concepts in this session are most needed when a leader is located at the intersection of multiple choice-points.
2. Sagen provides Joe with a good leadership skill, namely, remaining calm when things are urgent. He does this by explaining the concept of going third person.
3. He speaks directly to the concepts of Technical versus Adaptive Leadership.
4. He pushes Joe to have his team *Enter the Cone of Uncertainty*.
5. Sagen connects the three concepts of going third person, Adaptive Leadership, and *Enter the Cone of Uncertainty* by showing that they all are required when there is no clear pathway forward.
6. He suggests that Joe should have his team *Enter the Cone of Uncertainty*, and also to remain there for a while.
7. Sagen knows that *Entering the Cone of Uncertainty* is anxiety-inducing for Joe, and therefore when Joe does not set up another appointment, Sagen allows this. He knows it will be a long time before he sees Joe again.

Case Study:

1. Sagen presents the idea of going third person as a way of getting Joe to be less emotionally involved as he tries to address some business strategy issues. What other situations can you state in which the leader should go third person?
2. Have you been in a leadership situation where you were too emotionally involved and should have gone third person?
3. Can a leader go too far with going third person, and lose empathy? Under what circumstances is this most likely?
4. Adaptive Leadership is needed when the environment requires steps which the organization does not know how to take. Have you ever been in this situation? How did it go?
5. Can you describe a well-known company which failed to use Adaptive Leadership as its circumstance changed?
6. Can you describe a company which did use Adaptive Leadership and generated further success?
7. In the above two questions, please debate whether Technical vs. Adaptive Leadership was in play.
8. What does it mean to *Enter the Cone of Uncertainty*?
9. When is it most necessary to *Enter the Cone of Uncertainty*?
10. Shouldn't the CEO or top leader be responsible for the firm's strategy?
11. Joe is worried that *Entering the Cone of Uncertainty* will make him look like a weak leader. Is he right? How can he engage this process in a manner which allows him to look like a capable leader?
12. How far should he go in his questioning of his team? Once they all agree on a new strategy, should he encourage them to *Enter the Cone of Uncertainty* to look at how internal processes need to change, or should department heads just do that work independently?
13. How does Sagen know it will be a long time before he sees Joe again?

Chapter Four

Fourth Rite of Passage: The Space Between Us

Nearly a year has passed since Joe's last visit to Sagen. Not only has Joe not seen Sagen, but in fact, he has never even called him.

On this day, Joe is seated in Sagen's living room in the same seat and looking at the same mountains that he had so admired one year earlier. He can't help but notice how Sagen appears to have aged more than Joe had expected.

Joe begins, "Sagen, I give you my sincere apology for not calling or contacting you in the past year. I now know I was not ready to accept your counsel that my market had changed and therefore I needed to engage in Adaptive Leadership. Since then, the economy has shown slow improvement, but we win very few of the bids we submit. Our competition seems to always beat us. When I first came to see you, I had 75 employees. Now I have 45."

Joe continues, "One year ago, you said this was more than just a temporary problem and the dynamics of my market were changing rapidly. Secretly, I resisted your assessment of the situation. I believed I could return this company to prosperity once the economy would begin to improve. I also believed I could rally my employees toward rebuilding the Relationship Platform that my father once created and which generated prosperity for decades. My motive was simply to go back to the good old days. Now, I know the good old days are gone."

"Something else has changed," Joe says. "I am done blaming powerful forces outside myself for the poor performance of my enterprise. I am done externalizing. Other companies are successful in this environment and America continues to create a new batch of millionaires every year. There is prosperity to be had. I just need to stop blaming the environment and now I need to learn how to thrive in the world as it is."

Sagen says nothing. He listens.

Joe says, "During the past year we made all the right Technical Leadership moves and took the right steps to adjust to this difficult environment. I was lucky to have a great controller, who used her accounting skills to shed all the debt we could. She examined fixed versus variable expenses. The variable expenses were easy to reduce. However, the fixed expenses were more difficult. Still, she found ways to sell trucks that were sitting idle. Our warehouse was at half capacity and she found another company to rent part of our unused space."

Sagen asks, "So, your nose is above the waterline?"

"Yes, for now. Barely. I must tell you, this has been a very discouraging time regarding the manner in which our leadership team has conducted itself. As you had warned me, many of them blamed me directly for the downturn in our company. As this blaming went on and on, I recalled my conversations with you and worked hard not to take it too personally, to go third person. Your advice helped more than you can know."

Joe says, "As this dark chapter dragged on, the senior team seemed to split into three categories. First, there were some good people who simply came to work every day and ignored the internal politics. Second, there was a group who quietly but intensely campaigned against me. They opposed everything I suggested. They networked with one another at my expense."

Sagen asks, "And the third group?"

"The third group really consisted of just one person, Kathleen Anderson. This one was painful. Kathleen was my controller. During the entire time I worked with her, she became my trusted advisor and my confidant. I suppose it's not unusual for a company president to really become partners with his controller. There was a special kindness between us. She and her husband socialized with my wife and me. She was my sounding board for every new idea. What I didn't realize was that every idea I proposed was greeted with great flattery on her part. She would tell me my ideas were brilliant or that something I had done was genius. Of course, this fed my ego at a time when I was feeling pretty low. I soaked up that flattery. I liked her. More than anything, I trusted her.

"Then, two things happened. One day I left the office but returned much sooner than I had expected. I went to my office and worked quietly. I guess Kathleen didn't know I was there. Her door was open and I overheard a conversation between her and Stan Dwarsky, the leader of the internal opposition. She assured him I was lost, saying I had no viable plan going forward, and told him I am in no way the leader that my father was. They both laughed.

"Sagen, you have said I should not take these things personally but this one was personal. This was a betrayal and it injured me. Not only did I think Kathleen was my trusted advisor and partner, I thought she was my friend. But the pain did not stop there. A few weeks later I tried to increase our line of credit and the bank sent in an auditor. He found a consistent pattern of small amounts of money that had been taken from the company over the entire time I have been president. When I confronted her with this, she admitted it. I allowed her to resign."

Sagen speaks reassuringly, "Joe, you have been through a very difficult time. There is little I can say to reduce the pain of this betrayal."

Joe says, "I just feel like I was a naïve little boy. I was manipulated by her."

"Yes, in some ways you were naïve. When we first met, I could see there was a great deal of innocence about you. You were authentic and sincere. I think you were not taken by surprise that an opposition group emerged, but you were taken by surprise by Kathleen's betrayal. Now you can see, excessive flattery is just as lethal as excessive criticism. You are not the first leader to be ambushed by this.

"Joe, now you have some emotional work to do because of this betrayal. It will be your job to allow the loss of your innocence and to know this innocence has been replaced by wisdom. You are becoming seasoned in your leadership. You are becoming much more objective. From now on you will find it easier to go third person."

Joe replies, "I suppose I need to."

Sagen continues, "But Joe, I must ask, are you feeling either depressed or bitter?"

Joe looks at the floor. "Both. Very depressed and very bitter."

When Joe looks up, Sagen gains eye contact, "At some point, every leader has reason to be bitter and depressed. You must let go of all bitterness and depression. This bitter depression resides inside you and is a poison. It will destroy your ability to adapt and move forward. We all know people who have been injured many years earlier and remain stuck in their injury. Don't let that be you, Joe."

"Exactly how do I let these emotions go?"

"There are two things you must do. First you must forgive them all. Really, Joe. Forgive them. Forgive them many times over. Second, you must become successful and return prosperity to your company."

Sagen says, "This is an important passage in your journey toward becoming an extraordinary leader. You must accept your role as leader. You will probably have employees and teammates in the future whom you will regard as your friends. However, because of this experience with Kathleen, from this point forward, in those friendships you will automatically maintain just a little space between you and the other person. You must accept your injury here as part of your formation, a Rite of Passage. Allow this added wisdom to move you farther on your journey toward becoming an extraordinary leader. And you must accept that your relationship with these people is that of a leader and his followers."

Joe asks, "Is there more?"

"Yes, there is more. I said there are two things you must do. Once you come to a posture of forgiveness toward those who've injured you and your anger has receded, it will be time for you to re-engage so you can return to growth. Returning to growth and creating prosperity will fix much of this."

Joe says, "But I have been engaged. I have been giving it everything I've got."

Sagen instructs, "Yes you have, but I don't think you've come all this way to see me today so you can continue doing things the way you had been doing them in the past. The fact is, you have been at your firm two and a half years and at this moment your company is failing and so are you."

Joe pauses at the impact of these strong words. "Sagen, I can see you are right, but I don't know how to work differently. I don't see what I can do to dig out of this hole. I assure you, I am working on this as hard as I can. And I agree with you. I am failing."

Sagen says, "It is time for you to share your leadership burden with your teammates. Don't simply ask them to come up with a strategic plan, but ask them also to detail all the foreseeable steps in executing the plan. This has many names. People call it participative leadership, collaborative leadership, or shared leadership. Joe, you don't need to engage yourself more or try harder. You do need to engage your teammates. Take some of the weight off your shoulders and distribute it among your teammates. A good book would be the one by David Chrislip, titled *The Collaborative Leadership Fieldbook: A Guide for Citizens and Civic Leaders.* [5] Also, there are many good articles on this topic, such as the one by Craig L. Pearce and his colleagues [6] and a landmark article by Rosabeth Moss Kanter in Harvard Business Review. [7] You should read about this topic."

Sagen says, "We need to discuss something we talked about a year ago. This is exactly the kind of circumstance the Heifetz book says requires Adaptive Leadership. [4] Adaptive Leadership is needed when it seems there is no obvious path forward, or when there are multiple paths forward, but it is not clear which one your firm should choose."

"Joe, do you remember *Enter the Cone of Uncertainty*? You have been trying to avoid doing this by continuing to assume that you, as leader, must come up with the recovery plan. And so far, you haven't found one. Uncertainty is frightening, especially to a guy like you who is trained in mechanical engineering. Right?"

Joe replies, "Yes, I like to know how all the dominoes are going to fall before I tip over the first one. I've always been this way. I suppose that's why I chose mechanical engineering. It does make me anxious not to know."

Sagen asks, "Getting your senior team to *Enter Cone of Uncertainty* is a very awkward thing to do. Are you worried they will interpret this as weak leadership?"

"Yes, I do worry about that. There have been rumors that I'm not a good leader, so I am concerned that if I ask them to *Enter the Cone of Uncertainty* with me, my entire senior team will see me in a negative way. At this point, I don't think they value me as a leader or as a person, really."

Sagen replies, "Perhaps you are afraid you will lose their friendship or admiration. Please recall that you are still on your first mission, *Take the Lead*. In order to *Take the Lead* here, you should create a little space between you and the entire senior team. Just as you can become friends with a key teammate but still allow a little space between the two of you, so you can do the same with your senior team. This is your next Rite of Passage. I call it *The Space Between Us*. Building this skill will make you a much more impactful leader. It will reduce your need to seek so much approval from others.

"Joe, when we met a year ago I suggested your Rite of Passage was to *Enter the Cone of Uncertainty*. It is time now to allow yourself and your entire senior team to *Enter in the Cone of Uncertainty*. Well, actually don't just enter it. Reside there. Allow it to go on for as long as it needs to go on, while you and they work on the problem. As this process continues, the cone will get smaller and smaller, and a plan will emerge. Don't reach too soon for the plan. Allow the process to unfold."

Sagen continues, "I have a CEO friend in Kansas City who used to say that if you want to move up to the next level of anything,

'You've got to be comfortable being uncomfortable.' Every time his team had to create a new type of product or do something they didn't know how to do, he would tell them he understood that they were uncomfortable, but would say that if they couldn't learn to tolerate this discomfort, they would only remain in their old habits, skillsets, and products. He would tell them to become comfortable being uncomfortable." [12]

Sagen asks, "Joe, you have read *The Wisdom of Resilience Builders*. Do you remember what name that book has given to a turnaround plan?"

Joe replies, "The Hope Bearing Plan."

Sagen asks, "Good name for such a plan, yes?"

"Yes."

"Joe, there is just one more thing. I sense you have great urgency to return this company to health. Let me ask. If there were a board of directors who owned all the stock in this company and you worked for them, what timeframe would you give them regarding how fast this will happen?"

Joe replies, "As fast as humanly possible."

Sagen says, "Some advice from me, please. If there were such a board of directors, I would suggest you tell them this situation will get worse before it gets better because you and your team are required to address your market in a new way and you all have many new skills to develop. This will not happen overnight."

"And what shall I tell my employees?"

"Tell them the very same thing."

Sagen continues, "I hope to see you in one week. Between now and then I recommend you talk to your senior team about Adaptive Leadership and *Entering the Cone of Uncertainty*. Ask them to reside with you in that uncertainty while you and they work this problem together. It is time for shared leadership. It is time for a Hope Bearing Plan. And, Joe, as you begin this work, try to leave a slight buffer of safety between you and each of these key players. Remember, your new Rite of Passage here is called, *The Space Between Us*."

Joe's Rite of Passage:

1. Joe has been absent a long time because he is self-reliant and has felt a need to try to fix the firm his own way. Now he sees that he needs help. For the first time, he is truly receptive and coachable.

2. Joe experiences the reality that as the firm's finances degenerate, the internal climate degenerates along with it.

3. Like every leader, Joe should expect to experience a betrayal at some point. He is advised to use this experience to better develop his ability to go third person, now and in the future.

4. He must come to understand that as a result of this injury, his innocence has been replaced by wisdom. This gives him a future ability to become friends with his employees while still retaining a little space between himself and them.

5. Joe hears Sagen tell him to redevelop his organization within the framework of shared leadership.

6. After great struggle, Joe is receptive to the advice to ask his senior team to *Enter the Cone of Uncertainty* and to take the time to develop a Hope Bearing Plan together.

7. This Rite of Passage is called *The Space Between Us*. It has two layers. First, Joe is learning not to become too personally involved with key teammates. Second, creating a little space between Joe and his senior team will allow him to require them to *Enter the Cone of Uncertainty* without his becoming too emotionally taxed by their anxiety or resistance.

Sagen's Mentoring Process:

1. As Joe begins the session with an apology, Sagen neither criticizes nor condemns. He had greatly challenged Joe in their last session and is not surprised by this long absence.

2. Sagen also knows the work of some passages must be approached several times before the aspiring leader will competently address it.

3. Masterfully, Sagen again uses silence as an important interviewing skill.

4. When Joe describes Kathleen Anderson's betrayal, Sagen offers support but no superficial advice.

5. Sagen instructs that perhaps Joe has lost some innocence here and has replaced it with wisdom which will serve him well in the future.

6. Sagen advises that Joe must discard any depression or bitterness. Every leader has reason to be depressed and bitter. The two-pronged path to recovery is through forgiveness and a return to prosperity. In saying this, Sagen offers valuable advice.

7. Despite the one-year absence, Sagen sees that the corporate strategy of Joe's firm is exactly where it was when he last saw him. He encourages Joe to prompt his senior team to *Enter the Cone of Uncertainty*.

8. By suggesting that Joe should share the burden with his colleagues, Sagen introduces Joe to the concept of shared leadership. He recommends that Joe ask his team to collectively derive a Hope Bearing Plan.

9. The Hope Bearing Plan should be more than a simple change of strategy. Joe must get his leaders involved in how the plan will be executed.

10. Sagen offers Joe sage advice to always allow a little space between himself and his senior team. This is his next Rite of Passage. *The Space Between Us* will give him the courage to function well as a leader and it will help him avoid emotional injury as he does so.

Case Study:

1. Sagen says to Joe, "The fact is, you have been at your firm two and a half years and at this moment your company is failing and so are you." These are strong words. Was this appropriate for Sagen to say? Joe already knows he is failing. What is the value of this confrontation? When is this appropriate?

2. During his first meeting with Joe long ago, Sagen studied Joe's personality. Which combination of Joe's personality traits might explain Joe's absence? Which would explain why he has tried to fix the firm during this year without Sagen's help?

3. Have you ever been too self-reliant as you tried to lead? As time has passed, have you changed this pattern of behavior? If so, what set of circumstances caused you to alter this behavior pattern?

4. Do you believe this self-reliance is a natural tendency in most leaders? Why or why not?

5. Sagen does not seem frustrated that Joe absented himself all this time, nor does he seem frustrated as he re-explains the basics of *Entering the Cone of Uncertainty*. What do you think Sagen tells himself that allows him to remain so supportive as he does the same work with Joe for a second time?

6. In your supervision of others, have you had to go over the same material several times? Were you able to remain calm and supportive or did you become frustrated and let your frustration show?

7. Are there some supervisees who will change their behavior if you go over the material several times and others who won't? What are the possible personality traits of these two groups?

8. Sagen adds the concept of shared leadership and suggests Joe have the team outline the operational steps to execute the new strategy once it emerges.

9. Does every leader experience betrayal along the way?

10. When subordinates are friendly or kindly toward a leader, how can the leader know if this is sincere or manipulative?

11. Is it necessary for innocence to be destroyed so one can gain wisdom?

12. Sagen suggests forgiveness. Can Joe just forgive Kathleen Anderson one time and be done with it? How many times will he need to forgive her in order to unburden himself of the anger?

13. How would returning the firm to prosperity help Joe reduce the injury Kathleen has caused?

Chapter Five

Fifth Rite of Passage: Take the Lead

One week later, after Joe takes his seat Sagen slowly walks to a side table and brings Joe a pastry on a small plate. He asks if Joe would like coffee.

Joe, a little surprised at this level of hospitality, says, "Actually, I would love a cup of coffee."

Joe takes a bite of the light, fluffy pastry and says, "Wow. This is the best pastry I've ever had. May I ask what it is?"

"The French pastry is called vol-au-vent. A client of mine flew in yesterday from Paris and gave me a small box of them."

Joe takes a sip of the coffee and says, "Wow again. This coffee is amazing."

Sagen says, "It is from Ethiopia."

With honest sincerity, Joe asks, "Did someone fly in from Ethiopia?"

Sagen smiles, "No, Joe. I bought it at a local coffee shop."

They both chuckle.

Joe begins, "You encouraged me to take the weight off my shoulders and share it with my team. We are still a small firm, and I have only five people who report to me. My style of leadership all along has been to solve problems by speaking with each of them individually."

Joe continues, "I called a meeting, and in some ways it was successful, but the meeting showed me there are more leadership skills that I still need to develop. The successful piece was that I told my team our old way of doing things must change. The market in which we reside has shifted and our company is barely surviving. To my surprise, they all agreed something must change. However, they didn't agree on anything else.

"I told them that although I have some good ideas about what we should do, these problems are too big and complex for one man to solve, so we must work together to find adequate solutions. I said I need their expertise. I told them they should try to be comfortable being uncomfortable with the fact that at this moment we do not have a clear plan about what the future will look like.

"At that moment I felt great. I had said what I needed to say. However, that's when the real problems began. Each person in the room proposed that our poor performance was caused by someone else in the room. What followed was a rambling discussion in which I attempted to keep the meeting civil. Really, we got nothing accomplished and I just watched my team further disintegrate."

Sagen begins his work by asking, "Joe, did everyone attend this meeting?"

"No. Ron Bishop, our warehouse manager, sent a message at the last minute that he had an urgent personnel problem and would not be able to attend."

Sagen asks, "Did they all remain engaged during the entire meeting?"

"Well, yes and no. Jim Williams, our safety manager, was scribbling something in a notebook during the whole meeting. I believe he was reconciling monthly reports. However, Jane Davis is our new vice president of sales and she was highly engaged and exceptionally focused."

Sagen asks further, "Was there any work assigned for your next meeting?"

"Actually, we don't have a next meeting scheduled. And, no, I didn't assign any tasks."

Sagen speaks. "This recent history reminds us that you are still on your first mission, *Take the Lead*. Within that mission we have now encountered your newest Rite of Passage. I call it, *Take the Lead*. I can tell by the way you describe this meeting that you are pleased there was a meeting at all. You have not been having regular meetings with your senior team. Simply having a meeting is a step forward."

Joe says, "So, the name of the Right of Passage is the same as the name of this first mission, *Take the Lead*?"

"Yes, although you and your team must remain in the *Cone of Uncertainty*, it would be wise for you, as the leader, to provide some structure to this process. *Take the Lead*. This means you should have regularly scheduled meetings. They should start on time and end on time. Always. You should put out an agenda beforehand and provide minutes afterward. As they talk about problems, look for ways you can assign tasks to them. Then you should conduct a supervisory loop by following up. They should be told they will be expected to report progress in every subsequent meeting. At the end of each meeting, you should remind them when the next meeting will be.

"I also recommend, in addition to a one-hour-long weekly senior team meeting, you should have ten-minute stand-up meetings in your office with your entire senior team every morning. Everyone should be required to attend. No excuses. If they are traveling, they should phone in or video conference. This meeting is simply a forum for each manager to update the others about what's going on. A wonderful book titled *The Advantage* calls these meetings, The Daily Check In. This would be a vitally important book for you to read. It talks about how to form a healthy senior team." [13]

Joe objects, saying, "I'm not trying to resist here, but you say we should dwell in the *Cone of Uncertainty*. How can I assign tasks and have all these meetings if we are uncertain about what to do?"

Sagen says, "I do understand what you're saying. There is more. In your efforts to *Take the Lead*, I think a group your size should have annual planning sessions, perhaps two days in length, and follow those up with quarterly half-day planning sessions.

"One more thing, Joe. You should find a book or article about how to conduct a meeting. Choose any book or article you wish and follow the guidelines carefully. In order to *Take the Lead*, you will need all of this structure."

Joe says, "I know you are right, but that doesn't sound like me. That's not my style. It would seem strange for me to conduct myself in this way."

Sagen replies, "I know, Joe, operating this way would be a stretch for you. I'm not suggesting you treat your people in an unkind way or become overly dominant. I am simply suggesting you engage some leadership basics and execute them well."

Sagen says, "When life calls on us to act in a way that is foreign to how we see ourselves, sometimes it is best if we imitate another person who is highly skilled in this way. Try to think of a leader you have known who is well organized, has a schedule of meetings, uses an agenda, starts on time, ends on time, and assigns tasks. Then, pretend you're an actor, and play his or her role. You become that leader. You walk into the room the way he or she would. You start the meeting the way he or she would. You assign tasks the way he or she would. I recommend you read a book published by Harvard Business Review Press, *Act Like a Leader, Think Like a Leader.* [8]

"This is another Rite of Passage, Joe. For you to become an extraordinary leader, you must develop your skills at executing leadership basics. That's why this Rite of Passage is called, *Take the Lead.* This does not mean you should do their work for them. You should still ask them to come up with the Hope Bearing Plan, but it is your job to insist on meetings and give them assignments. Then you should follow-up.

"I assure you if you do these things, eventually they will become quite natural to you. Your team will function more effectively. Even more important, these meetings, the assigned tasks, the follow-up, and all of this will provide a structure within which your team will begin to operate comfortably. It is inside this structure that your team will find its adaptive answers."

Joe's Rite of Passage:

1. In this Rite of Passage Joe is presented with the idea that he must *Take the Lead*.
2. He should stop trying to solve problems by having informal conversations with his team members.
3. In order to be a leader, he must don the garb of a leader, walk, talk, and think like a leader.
4. To *Take the Lead* he should create a schedule of structured meetings and get real work done in them.
5. It is time for Joe to execute leadership basics like having an agenda for meetings, starting on time, and ending on time. After each meeting, minutes should be sent out.
6. Joe hears that tasks should be assigned and then he should take steps to appropriately follow-up.
7. Joe listens as Sagen recommends having daily ten-minute stand-up meetings.
8. This Rite of Passage is called, *Take the Lead*. For Joe to become an extraordinary leader, he must lead much more actively.

Sagen's Mentoring Process:

1. Sagen begins the session by increasing his personal connection with Joe. He offers him specialty pastries and coffee as if Joe were a guest in his home.

2. He congratulates Joe for placing the responsibility of developing a plan on the shoulders of his team. However, Sagen is not surprised that these team members are unable to accept this responsibility. Instead, they argue and blame each other.

3. It becomes clear that Joe's leadership style is too unstructured. One team member does not show for the meeting, another scribbles paperwork, Joe gives no assignments, and he does not set a date for the next meeting.

4. Sagen directs Joe to *Take the Lead*. This means he must arrange structured meetings that start on time, end on time, have assignments, and involve follow up.

5. Sagen is aware that until now Joe has been externally focused on the people and events which surround him. Sagen observes a breakthrough when Joe tells him, "There are more leadership skills that I still need to develop." This tells Sagen that Joe is now fully focused on his own leadership development.

6. Sagen works to escort Joe into his next Rite of Passage, *Take the Lead*.

Case Study:

1. Do you think it was good procedure for Sagen to offer Joe gifts of French pastries and specialty coffee? Isn't Sagen supposed to be an objective third party? Doesn't this gift increase their personal connection? Please discuss your answer, pro and con.

2. As you look at how Joe approached the work of getting his team to *Enter the Cone of Uncertainty*, (e.g., "I have some good ideas…" "We must work together") do you feel he handled it well?

3. Joe is surprised that his first real meeting to select an adaptive strategy disintegrated into blaming and chaos. However, Sagen does not seem surprised. Are you surprised by the team's behavior? Have you had a similar experience?

4. Should Joe have expected his senior team to be able to competently address the firm's strategic needs during their first meeting?

5. Does it seem as if Sagen is putting pressure on Joe when he asks questions such as whether everyone attended this meeting, remained engaged, and got any work assigned?

6. Joe seems to resist moving from his informal leadership style toward a more structured approach. Why would this be difficult? Have you had to do this? If so, what difficulties did you encounter? If you haven't done this, should you?

7. Is the commencement of these structured meetings a way of communicating to the senior team that Joe is the boss? If so, is that a good thing?

8. How should Joe handle it if he sees Jim Williams reconciling monthly reports during a meeting? How would you handle it? Would you have difficulty being assertive? Might you be too assertive?

Second Mission: Create Followers

The Four Passages of the
Second Mission: Create Followers

7. Respond to Followers' Changing Needs

8. Transformational Leadership

9. Get Them All to Be All In

6. Create Followers

Chapter Six

Sixth Rite of Passage: Create Followers

One week later Sagen asks, "So, tell me Joe. Is there any progress to report?"

Joe seems somehow more relaxed. He says, "Well, I have absolutely no progress to report regarding my team. However, I have great progress to report regarding myself."

"Oh, how so?"

"I have done three things to help me *Take the Lead*. First, I have set up a schedule of meetings for our senior team and asked each of them to begin having regular meetings in their own departments. I have instructed them these meeting always will have an agenda, start on time every time, end on time, and leave with assignments. This still feels a little strange, but we will get used to it.

"Second, I have mentioned Stan Dwarsky to you. He was our most tenured salesperson and had been a long-time employee of my father. I've known him since I was a boy. He, however, was the leader of the internal opposition. He is the man whose conversation with Kathleen Anderson I overheard. As it turns out, he has continued to have similar and even more derogatory conversations with many other people. I called him into my office and told him I had asked to speak with him because I was going to terminate him. I began by listing out many of his great accomplishments. I reminded him that I have known him since I was very young. I told him I appreciated all the years of his good service and said he was a senior employee who handled most of our key accounts. Then I told him I was aware of the many negative conversations he had had with people throughout the company and that one customer had reported a similar conversation. I told him I did not trust him anymore, and I wished him the best of luck. We shook hands and he left.

"During the interview I'm sure I appeared calm, but I was not. My level of personal upset came as a surprise to me. I remained calm flying helicopters into dangerous places but not while I was firing this man. After he left my office I sat behind my desk and did nothing for about five minutes."

Sagen replies, "Joe, you flew those dangerous combat missions to save people. You are a helper. You were not trying to save Stan. He was injured by this conversation. Still, you did the right thing because you have a responsibility to the many other lives under your leadership. Firing someone is a difficult thing to do. I hope it never becomes easy for you, even if it is so justified."

Joe says, "Okay, I'm sure you are right. There was a third thing I did to *Take the Lead*. I called a meeting of the entire senior team and told them we would be working together to turn our company around. I told them our first meeting would be a long one so we set it up for an evening. Prior to going into this meeting, I decided I needed to go third person. I remembered how I was quite skilled at setting my emotions aside when I was a medevac pilot. I promised myself I would do the same here. I believed going third person would allow me to objectively observe the group process and would help me not to take any insults or criticisms personally. I also recalled you had suggested I pretend to be you. So, rather than tell them where our company is and what it is, I asked.

"Sagen, everyone in the room seemed anxious and off guard because, once I asked each question, I did not immediately answer it myself. I allowed them to wallow in their anxiety and I made them work for every answer. I have observed that you do that to me."

Sagen smiles and nods.

"I asked the team to describe our current situation. I found their answers clustered into two groups. First, there were those who minimized the current situation and pointed to a few minor victories we have recently achieved, such as getting a couple of small new accounts. Second, there were those who exaggerated the pain and seemed to be panicking.

"Up to this point, I refrained from offering my own opinion. I asked each person who responded to back up their response with data or information. This was my effort to get them to become more objective and to go third person themselves, more or less.

"I didn't use the phrase *Enter the Cone of Uncertainty*. However, I did tell them we must embrace the notion that these are uncertain times, and that we should not resist that uncertainty. I told them if we allow ourselves to share observations, ideas, and proposed solutions, this uncertainty would gradually reduce, and if we continue this process for a long enough time, together we can find a new way forward.

"I did share the idea of Adaptive Leadership and said that in times of uncertainty we may be required to discard our past practices and to develop new strategies.

"Sagen, I must say this approach only threw the group into deep chaos. I believe they wanted me to propose the perfect solution to all our problems. They were looking toward me for strong leadership. By suggesting we must swim in this pool of uncertainty for a while longer, and further suggesting we may need to do things very differently in the future, I saw that their anxiety was going up through the roof."

Sagen says, "I can see how this would happen."

Joe says, "My new controller, Marilyn Lewis, had tears coming down her face as she told me she and her business office staff could not work any harder. They are doing their best to get the bills out immediately and to delay payment on as many vendors as they can. She couldn't imagine what more I could expect from her.

"My warehouse manager, Ron Bishop, started shouting. He said he, too, was unable to work any harder. He said our current warehousing system is pure pandemonium and we have crates and boxes strewn all over the place. We have trucks arriving to be loaded when we don't know what items to put on them, and we have been getting a stream of customer complaints about wrong parts and orders. In response to their comments, rather than making an attempt to fix this, I only suggested that everything Marilyn and Ron had said is further evidence that we need input from everyone in order to find the right new direction. Then they all just stared at me."

Sagen says, "I am very impressed that you didn't offer a solution at that point."

Joe says, "Actually, even as their emotional level went up, I remained calm. When you and I started our meeting today, I told you that I had no progress to report regarding the group, but I had good progress to report regarding myself. I felt like I was functioning as a leader at that moment. I was placing the responsibility for designing the next chapter of our lives on them, and they didn't like it. Still, I knew this was the work we needed to do. I held their feet to the fire. I felt strong and confident through the entire meeting. For me, this is great progress."

"Joe, I believe you did an excellent job of strengthening your leadership skills in this meeting. You *Took the Lead* by making them do the work and not jumping in yourself to rescue them. And it seems you left a little space between you and your team."

Sagen instructs, "You have said your group did not make progress, but I must disagree. I think you have more to tell me about this meeting. However, I must interject something at this moment. The reaction you received from this group has a name. A psychologist would call it an initial response to shock. It is similar to the way people react when a doctor tells them they have a terrible diagnosis. Some people cry, some get angry, and some just remain quiet. All of these reactions, which you observed, indicate that they heard you and they understand you have shared work to do together. They fear taking on this responsibility. I regard this to be great progress."

Joe says, "Hmmm, that is a very interesting way to look at it. Can we suppose they have now *Entered the Cone of Uncertainty*?"

"Precisely so, Joe. Precisely so."

Joe says, "I allowed this unfocused discussion to go on for about a half hour without giving much input from me. Eventually, I began to ask them more focused questions. I told them we were built on the Relationship Platform. I explained this meant we know our customers well, that we are eager to do favors, and that we seek long-term attachment more than simply seeking financial return. Our relationship with our customers is more than a transaction. However, I told them there are three other competitive platforms and I described them.

"I asked them which platform describes our customers' overall industries today. I was quite impressed with how insightful their answers were. They didn't use the exact words I will now, but they described our changing environment in great detail. First, they focused on the automobile industry and said that in the 1920s when Henry Ford built the first mass production assembly lines, he caused the car industry to become Efficient Platform. However, in the 1980s, the American car manufacturers had no competitive platform at all. They weren't efficient. They weren't creative. They just made cars. Their manufacturing processes were slow and wasteful, and some of those cars had poor quality. That's when highly efficient Japanese manufacturers like Toyota took over the market. These American firms lost their competitive intent and that created Toyota's opportunity to shine. Sagen, my team told me all of this.

"The second thing they said was that in recent years much of America's biggest mass production work has moved overseas where labor is cheaper. Ron Bishop called it mindless manufacturing, like making lug nuts and door hinges. He said manufacturing of complex systems like conveyors has remained in America. However, he quickly admitted that overseas manufacturers are getting better at complex manufacturing.

"I asked them how many family-owned small manufacturers had gone out of business or moved overseas in the past five years. They seemed to agree it was about 30%. I asked if they believed all U.S. small manufacturers are going to disappear. They suggested they will not. Then I asked, if our customer base is shrinking and the new growth market is Efficient Platform, shouldn't we be looking at how to address and serve an Efficient Platform industry?

"Sagen, they seemed to have no good ideas about how to begin doing this. However, their emotional level during this part of the meeting could best be described as calm.

"I'm not sure where to go with this group next to get them more fully engaged with creating a good outcome. They seemed to understand the problem, but they had no good ideas about what to do next. Also, I don't believe the entire team is *All In*. I sense they have high anxiety but not a high level of commitment."

Sagen seems to be in deep thought for a moment. He says, "You have greatly strengthened your leadership skills during your first mission, *Take the Lead*. However, you have not created strong followership among your people. It is time for you to begin your second mission. This mission has four Rites of Passage. The name of the mission is the same as the name of its first Rite of Passage; *Create Followers*."

Sagen begins instructing, "To *Create Followers* you must begin by attempting to understand their fear and pain. Most leaders examine a time like this through their own eyes and describe it in terms of their own pain. Extraordinary leaders are good at understanding the pain, frustration, suffering, and needs of their followers. In fact, in order for these people to become your followers, you must carefully study their needs. Then you must communicate that you understand their needs. Finally, you and they together must craft a plan that your followers believe will meet their needs. Only then will they become your followers. Only then will they fully engage in solving this problem with you.

"I have some books to recommend. First, I recommend you read *Making Sense of Change Management* by Esther Cameron and Mike Green. [9] This book is in its fifth edition, and it is one of the most important change management books in the profession. It calls the leader a change agent. Pay special attention to the places in which this book creates a political metaphor to understand change. To achieve change, a leader must resolve the multiple, conflicting, and complex variables that will be impacted by any decision he or she makes. These variables must be considered on behalf of all persons and subgroups who would be impacted. Every decision you make as you promote change within your organization will impact some people positively and other people negatively. Cameron and Green say quite directly, 'there will be winners and losers' (p. 106). You should understand this and strive to balance the needs of each group. Successfully balancing the conflicting needs of these various groups is an art form, well mastered by extraordinary leaders as they work to *Create Followers*."

Sagen persists, "The second book I recommend is among my top five favorite books on leadership. It is by James MacGregor Burns and is simply titled, *Leadership*.[10] This book is substantial and gives us a deep theory of power dynamics in leadership. It has some gravity to it, so you should take your time reading it. James MacGregor Burns has great credibility. He has won the Pulitzer Prize and The National Book Award.

"Of greatest importance to you is MacGregor Burns' discussion of how leaders collect the support of various constituencies of followers. In fact, the only source of their leadership power is in the two-way attachment between the leader and the followers he or she collects. In your company there are several different constituencies. You might call them designers, mechanics, salespeople, administrative staff, warehouse employees, or something else. MacGregor Burns states that great leaders immerse themselves in each constituency, so they can most effectively learn the needs of each group of people. The effort involved in this learning process creates a bond between the leader and the constituency. It also educates the leader about what his or her people really need. Becoming skilled at this will greatly aid you as you *Create Followers*."

Sagen says, "So, the notion of constituencies ties in with Cameron and Green's suggestion that every change-causing choice the leader makes will cause some subgroups to be winners and others to be losers. Be aware of who is losing. Don't avoid their pain. Go to it. Address it compassionately with them. This concept of winners and losers is also discussed in the Heifetz book. [3]

"MacGregor Burns is talking about politicians and government leaders, so he calls them constituencies. In the business world we call them stakeholders. Constituencies and stakeholders come in groups. A good leader seeks their support. You should ask yourself if there were an election at KC Miller Conveyor a year from now for the office of president, how many of your people would vote for you. This does not mean you are in a popularity contest, but it does mean they would vote for you if they think you are striving to meet their needs and if they believe you are competent.

"MacGregor Burns' book says some surprising things. For example, he points to Chinese Premier Mao Zedong as one of history's greatest leaders. Stated more accurately, MacGregor Burns says Mao was a great leader in his early career as he gained power. After that, he became a tyrant and killed millions of people to retain his control of the country. MacGregor Burns says tyrants simply exercise raw power. He says tyranny is not the same thing as leadership. However, Mao's early work with rural peasants in the 1920s and 1930s opened his eyes to the extreme suffering of these people. He lived among them and worked alongside them. He watched as their children starved to death. He moved about the different provinces so he could learn and connect. China still had an unfair economic system with those at the top absorbing all the benefit. This unfair economic system fueled Mao's Chinese Communist Revolution. Mao used his knowledge of their suffering to gain followers. He promised them bread, land, and prosperity. This strengthened his own political position and he developed immense popularity among the Chinese peasants as a result. At first, they became his followers because they loved him. Later, they became his subjects because they feared him.

"As you work to understand your people's needs, you must be aware that there is a hierarchy of needs. This is a concept most notably pioneered by the famous Abraham Maslow in his 1954 book, *Motivation and Personality*. [11] This book is still relevant today. In it,

Maslow proposes that needs can be arranged from most basic to most sophisticated. He offers the following model."

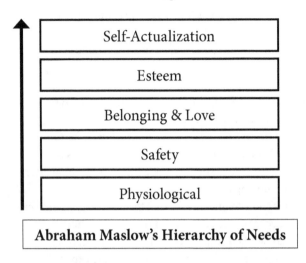

Abraham Maslow's Hierarchy of Needs

Sagen was nearly done with this lesson. "Joe, we have covered a lot of material today. I must tell you, I am enormously impressed with the good work you are doing. You are not the same man who sat before me one week ago looking somewhat lost and feeling helpless. You're up on your feet and exercising good leadership skills. You have made great progress on the Rite of Passage we discussed last week, *Take the Lead*. I say bravo to you.

"I will ask you to do three things. First, continue your work with your team while you all make your way through the *Cone of Uncertainty* together. A good process has begun there. Second, read as much as you can of the books I have recommended. And third, carefully study the needs of each group of your stakeholders. As you study these needs, you might take Maslow's model and insert your own list on it, which reflects your team's needs.

"Your new mission has the same name as your new Rite of Passage, *Create Followers*. I've given you a lot to do. Let's meet in three weeks."

Joe's Rite of Passage:

1. Joe continues his work from the previous Rite of Passage, *Take the Lead*.
2. He does this first by establishing a schedule of competently run meetings.
3. His second step to *Take the Lead* is the termination of a key employee who has become subversive within the organization.
4. Joe tells Sagen that as a third step in his effort to *Take the Lead*, he has prompted his senior team to *Enter the Cone of Uncertainty*, handed the strategic problem to them, has asked them to create a turnaround plan, and has made his own personal efforts to go third person during the process.
5. Joe has come to understand that the team will become more primitive and disorganized in its initial response to shock.
6. Joe has worked to get his senior team to honestly address the real challenge. In this case it is a strategic shift in their marketplace, in which the customers are seeking much more efficiency.
7. During this meeting with Sagen, Joe learns that as he leads through change, he must become skilled at balancing various constituents' opposing needs. He must detect which stakeholders will gain and lose as he makes each decision.
8. He will study Maslow's Hierarchy of Needs and revise it to fit his team's needs.
9. Joe's new Rite of Passage is to *Create Followers* by understanding and meeting his people's needs. He hears Sagen tell him that as he seeks to understand his followers' needs and as he demonstrates that he accepts their needs, this will create a bond between him, as leader, and his followers. All these leadership processes will help him *Create Followers*.

Sagen's Mentoring Process:

1. Sagen congratulates Joe for patiently allowing his teammates to display great anxiety in their initial response to shock. He is pleased that Joe does not rescue them.
2. Sagen can see they have joined Joe in *Entering the Cone of Uncertainty*.
3. Sagen praises Joe for focusing their attention on their changed strategic environment and for seeking their input. This causes them to become calm and objective.
4. Sagen comments that Joe has made great strides in his leadership but now he must begin his next mission and Rite of Passage, *Create Followers*.
5. He recommends three books which show how every decision creates constituencies of winners and losers, how a leader's power is derived from the two-way attachment with followers, and the role of Maslow's Hierarchy of Needs.
6. Sagen gives Joe a huge reading assignment and also asks him to rework Maslow's Hierarchy.
7. Sagen knows that all this work will create a framework which will help Joe achieve this Rite of Passage, which is to *Create Followers*.
8. Sagen is aware that Joe's attachment to him is increasing. A manifestation of this is Joe having said, "I also recalled you had suggested I pretend to be you." Joe's statement is inaccurate. In the previous session, Sagen simply suggested Joe think of a competent leader and imitate him or her.

Case Study:

1. Joe has created an aggressive schedule of meetings for the senior team and every department. Is this always necessary? Is it overkill? Can't a small or midsized business operate informally?

2. What does the termination of Stan Dwarsky contribute toward Joe's ability to *Take the Lead*? Does it give him credibility as the boss, or will people now fear for their jobs? Please argue both sides.

3. His third step is to make his team *Enter the Cone of Uncertainty*. Why should Joe expect it to work this time when it failed a year ago?

4. Joe's senior team was able to speak quite frankly about the shift toward more efficiency occurring now in all manufacturing industries. Why were they not able to articulate this a year earlier? What might have changed?

5. Regarding the requirement to balance various teammates' needs, which stakeholders will gain and which will lose if Joe shifts his firm toward greater efficiency? Is it possible to make these changes without anyone losing in any way?

6. What if no one loses his or her job, but after this firm shifts toward operating more efficiently, everyone will be required to do many things differently? Is this a loss which needs balancing? What might an effort to balance the needs of these winners and losers look like?

7. Sagen advises Joe to pour some energy into understanding each stakeholder's needs in order to *Create Followers*. Then Joe should communicate that he understands those needs. Are there other ways to build followership? How would this be done?

8. What if Joe does understand that some teammates will be required to work very differently in the future and then he shows these people that he understands how difficult this will be for them? What if the teammates still don't want to see this change happen? Would this mean Joe has failed to *Create Followers*?

9. Maslow's hierarchy has been around for approximately 70 years. Is it outdated? Is it too simple? Why would Sagen use it here?

10. What needs will Joe discover as he uses Maslow's hierarchy as a framework to understand his own employees' needs? Please brainstorm this question before reading the next chapter.

Chapter Seven

Seventh Rite of Passage: Respond to Followers' Changing Needs

The front door opens as Joe climbs the porch steps. Sagen shakes Joe's hand but doesn't turn to go inside. Instead, he inhales deeply and exhales slowly. He says, "Joe, let's take a moment and breathe this fresh mountain air."

Joe takes it all in. It is just as spellbinding to him now as it had been the first time he came to Sagen's home. The mountains are majestic and the sky is the richest blue.

Once inside, Joe takes his usual seat and says, "Sagen, I have a lot to report. I had expected our team to remain in chaos for a long time. I had thought that I would need to continuously remind them it is okay to be uncomfortable, but things have changed quickly. As you remember, Ron Bishop had been quite angry and quite verbal a few weeks ago. However, most recently he surprised me by saying the only thing he was uncomfortable with was my asking them to meet once per week to find our new strategy. He suggested we meet three times per week.

"Everyone on my senior team agreed. This all occurred the day after I last visited you. At that time, we set up three two-hour meetings each week. However, we used only two of those meetings before we found our new strategy. In the first meeting, there was 100% consensus that our old way of doing business is outdated. We have lost our place in a market that has moved on without us. We should put everything under the microscope. Nothing should be sacred. Jane Davis, our sales vice president, said we should start by asking what John Dillinger would say in this situation."

Sagen asks, "John Dillinger?"

Joe continues, "When they asked Dillinger why he robbed banks he said it was because that's where the money is. Jane said we must begin by asking where the money is in our market, which groups of customers have dropped us, and in which segments of our market we expect to see growth."

"Good logic," says Sagen.

Joe says, "We were still in the *Cone of Uncertainty*, but that cone had just narrowed greatly. What followed was an enthusiastic and spirited discussion in which the entire team concluded that our customers could be divided into two segments, small to medium and large. Of course, there are other ways to divide our customer segments, but this one made the most sense. As our conversation continued, Jane said we used to win about 60% of our bids to large manufacturers, but this has dropped to around 30%. Further, she said we seem not to have lost ground with our small manufacturers. However, no one in the room could explain why our sales success rate had been cut in half with big manufacturers. We simply had no way of understanding this."

"Was the team ready to put some of this into action?" asks Sagen.

"We announced that our Hope Bearing Plan was to learn what had happened with large manufacturers and to aggressively pursue them. Sagen, in just two meetings we created a Hope Bearing Plan, and it is a good one.

"I took your advice and I made an assignment. I asked Jane to choose three salespeople and assign one to car companies, one to food and beverage manufacturers, and one to government agencies like the post office. They were to do nothing other than dig in and help us understand why we have fallen out of favor. To everyone's surprise, all three came back with the same explanation."

Sagen asks, "And what was that explanation?"

Joe answers, "Well, let's talk about the auto industry. You have previously told me that in the past decade the Japanese car companies have been using LEAN processes to increase efficiencies, reduce waste, and cut manufacturing cost. My team reported that LEAN methodology completely explains why the Japanese are so impressively outpacing the American car companies. It is their secret weapon. It turns out LEAN processes also include suppliers. The American car companies were slow to change their ways and finally they realized this was the reason they were losing so badly to the Japanese, so now they are implementing LEAN in a big way. LEAN process improvements are happening inside their factories, but the car companies haven't stopped there. They also have been giving extensive LEAN training to their suppliers. This has created a partnership between the car companies and their suppliers, and we are not in on that partnership."

Sagen asks, "Is it possible for you to simply be a Relationship Platform supplier, as you always have been, and still succeed in this environment?"

"I don't think so. The world has changed and we've been left behind. What the customer wants from us is extreme speed and remarkable accuracy. They also want just-in-time supplies, which means many suppliers are building their own plants adjacent to the car companies' factories. This is moving fast.

"We need to look at everything completely differently. Of course, we want car companies as clients, but we also need to partner with the car companies' other suppliers and show how our conveyor systems will help them with their own speed and agility. We need to build conveyors which separate and move parts that have never been touched by human hands. We think many of our competitors have begun to address this issue, but none have truly mastered the new set of skills needed here. We think we can outpace them quickly. We see it as nothing but opportunity.

"I took your advice about winners and losers among our stakeholder groups, so I had a meeting with all our salespeople. I was afraid those who would be staying with small and mid-range manufacturers would view themselves as the losers as I began to assign greater resources to the large customer group when we made this strategy shift. I assured them we would not leave them behind."

Sagen says, "I am impressed, Joe, truly impressed."

Joe says, "Thank you. I feel I am on the right track, but I delayed for a long time. Something else has happened that has greatly surprised me. The mood among all employees in our firm is remarkably positive. They are smiling and happy. I never realized that having a credible Hope Bearing Plan would so improve the internal climate, but it has. In so many ways, it seems I have solved my problems."

Sagen has listened carefully. Now he begins his work. "Well, Joe, I must say again how impressed I am. You have exercised impressively competent leadership here and it is producing remarkable early results. However, I must ask, can we say your work with me is done? You have *Taken the Lead*, developed strong basic leadership skills, engaged your team in Adaptive Leadership, left some *Space Between Us* as you *Entered the Cone of Uncertainty*, developed a Hope Bearing Plan, attempted to establish balance among your stakeholders, and *Created Followers* by meeting their need for prosperity. That is significant progress. So, are we done?"

Joe studies Sagen for a moment. He waits, then he replies. "Sagen, you once asked me if I want to be an extraordinary leader. Despite this good progress I think I am somewhere mid-journey. You have told me there are four missions and each one has its own Rites of Passage. You have told me there are many passages that I must travel through in order to build myself up to the level of being an extraordinary leader. Clearly, I am not sure-footed enough to claim that title yet."

Sagen holds his smile for a long time as he looks at his prodigy. "Good, Joe. Then let's get to work."

Sagen asks, "Did you have time to look at any of the books I recommended?"

Joe replies, "I have been reading all of them. You have turned me into a graduate student. I read in bed. I read in the bathroom. I tried to read in the shower, but it didn't really work. When my wife and I go somewhere, I ask her to drive so I can read in the car. Do you think maybe I'm overdoing it?"

"No. You once told me you are *All In* and people's lives are now depending on you. If you want to lead, you have to read."

"Well, I am reading."

Sagen continues, "May I ask? What have you done with Maslow's Hierarchy of Needs?"

Joe says, "Well, I spent a great deal of time thinking about the needs all my people might have. I added more than Maslow originally had. Here they are."

Self-Actualization	↑	Help the individual to become an expert within the group. Allow the person to develop new occupational interests.
Esteem	↑	Status within the group. Praise from the leader. Praise from peers. Achieving something difficult.
Belonging and Love	↑	Show them you care: Receiving kindness from teammates. Show them you care: Receiving kindness from the leader. Treat each other respectfully every day.
Safety	↑	We are safe from predators like competitors and market shifts.
Physiological	↑	Injury-free working environment. Retirement contributions. Health plan. Good pay.

Joe's Work on Maslow's Hierarchy of Needs

Sagen studies Joe's work carefully and silently. He runs his finger from the bottom of the page to the top very slowly. Eventually he begins to mumble to himself, quietly. Joe thinks Sagen is taking much too long for such a simple chart.

Without a word, Sagen stands up and leaves the room. When he returns, he is carrying a flip chart and two markers. With great speed he re-creates Joe's chart using a fine-tipped marker. However, Sagen leaves several blank spaces in the chart.

Sagen takes a broad-tipped marker and fills in the blank spaces. The new chart looks like this:

Self-Actualization	↑	**Strive toward a higher purpose.** Help the individual to become an expert within the group. Allow the person to develop new occupational interests. **Support the community through work with charities.** **Company becomes more socially responsible, externally.** **Company attempts to improve social & racial issues, internally.**
Esteem	↑	**Successfully accomplishing something difficult.** **Being included as a member of a group of competent people.** Status within the group. Praise from the leader. Praise from peers.
Belonging and Love	↑	**Company becomes a community.** **Experience the pride of being a member of a great team.** Show them you care: Receiving kindness from teammates. Show them you care: Receiving kindness from the leader. **Being known as a person, with a family, hobbies, interests, and moments of joy and sorrow.** Treat each other respectfully every day.
Safety	↑	**Trust that we are safe among each other, so we can speak openly, criticize new ideas, and improve processes without fear of repercussions.** We are safe from predators like competitors and market shifts.
Physiological	↑	Injury-free working environment. Retirement contributions. Health plan. Good pay.

Sagen's Work on Maslow's Hierarchy of Needs

Now it is Joe's turn to study the chart quietly. He reads it carefully. After what seems like a long time, he addresses Sagen.

"Sagen, I can see that your additions are extremely valuable. Thank you for each one of them. I must say, however, this chart has become so complex that I'm not sure where to begin. Together we have changed Maslow's five needs into 23 needs. Do I simply address them in sequence?"

Sagen speaks with great courtesy, "It is interesting that in his classic book, Abraham Maslow never said these needs must be addressed in sequence. He did suggest that higher-order needs are rarely addressed by the individual when lower order needs remain unfulfilled. The idea is that if a person is struggling for survival, he or she is likely to be unconcerned about poetry or art. However, this is not always true. History has shown that some of the greatest poets and artists lived in impoverished conditions. So, sometimes higher order needs can be addressed even when lower order needs are unfulfilled."

Joe asks, "Address them all at once?"

Sagen smiles. "That's not the idea, Joe. Think about it this way: If a man is starving to death and you take him into a great banquet hall with a table filled with food, he will approach the food. However, if the room then catches fire he will run away, momentarily neglecting his need for food. Some needs do come before others, but as a leader you should look to see which needs can be addressed simultaneously. Don't seek to address them all in sequence."

Joe says, "Clear as mud, Sagen. I will have to think about this one."

Sagen encourages, "Yes, please do give it great thought."

Joe continues, "You have said a good leader watches to see how the followers' needs change over time. Can you explain this a little more?"

Sagen says, "Yes, this is a good question because it points to the mission you are on now, *Create Followers*. It also points to your next Rite of Passage within that mission, which is to *Respond to Followers' Changing Needs*."

Sagen asks, "Do you recall I told you about Chinese Premier Mao Zedong and his work with peasants? He had a deep understanding of the peasants' needs and therefore a powerful attachment was created between him and the peasantry. When we look back today, it might appear to us that he was the undisputed leader of the Chinese Communist Revolution all along and effortlessly became premier. What we don't remember is that he had many rivals attempting to displace him along the way, but they did not understand the needs of the peasants the way he did, nor did they have this two-way attachment. He was masterful at gaining followership. So, he became their first leader.

"What happened subsequently is quite instructive. Having created a revolution, Mao was ready for a time of peace and prosperity, but subsequent insurrections began to occur in the provinces. He spent the remainder of his days suppressing opposition and resistance to his rule. What went wrong was quite simple. He knew the peasants needed bread and sustenance. He gave that to them. However, having reached this level of satisfaction, they wanted more. They wanted what today we would call a middle-class existence. Either he did not know this, or he did not know how to satisfy this need. This is why he stopped being a leader and began being a tyrant. He did not successfully *Respond to Followers' Changing Needs.*"

Sagen says, "Now let's compare Mao with an extraordinary leader, Nelson Mandela. As you know, Mandela was imprisoned for 27 years and during that time he became a pacifist. After his release he led his nation to end apartheid in South Africa. He became the country's first black president. This was monumentally historic. The overwhelming majority of South Africa's population is black, and Mandela knew they needed an end to their oppression. They also needed equal status and basic rights. He is credited with giving them all these things.

"Having addressed their basic needs, he then strove to meet higher-level needs. He set up medical clinics, even in rural and remote areas. He vastly improved public education. He worked to create an economic system that would allow hope to the entire population. And he suppressed resentment and retaliation through his Truth and

Reconciliation Commission, which was intended to instill a culture of forgiveness so the country could move forward. In his retirement he was revered and loved as an elder statesman until he died of old age."

Joe says, "So, after his people's needs were met at basic levels, he then worked to meet their new sets of needs. His leadership Rite of Passage was to *Respond to Followers' Changing Needs.*"

"Exactly, Joe. Needs, once met, then evolve. An extraordinary leader, like Nelson Mandela, is aware of this and works to address each new set of needs."

Joe asks, "Please tell me. How do I do this in my company?"

Again, Sagen smiles. He says, "You have already begun to move through this Rite of Passage. Do you remember the first time you gathered your senior team together and told them that the company was in trouble? Their reaction was to attack each other. However, when you gathered them together one year later and asked them to find a solution, they talked openly and safely among each other as they rallied to oppose a common enemy, your changing marketplace.

"You have not completed this Rite of Passage. Just because they spoke transparently and safely among each other without fear of retribution that one time does not mean this openness and mutual trust has become a permanent part of your culture. This is where you should begin. Your new Hope Bearing Plan has established a path to prosperity for the moment. Now they have developed a next-level need to solve problems with and among each other. They need each other. They need each other's expertise. Their needs are shifting to this new level."

"Your Rite of Passage here is to continue to develop your skill at detecting each next-level set of your employees' needs and then *Respond to Followers' Changing Needs.* This is a difficult Rite of Passage. You will need to return to it many times during your career."

Joe simply says, "Thank you for this, Sagen. Thank you."

Joe's Rite of Passage:

1. Joe comes to understand that his team should not be expected to enjoy *Entering the Cone of Uncertainty*. He is surprised to see that once he puts responsibility for change squarely on their shoulders, they find creative solutions quickly.
2. Often there is a newly formed positive climate immediately after a Hope Bearing Plan is established. Despite this positive mood, Joe refuses to be fooled into thinking his work is done.
3. An important part of Joe's Rite of Passage here is to know that once he satisfies a layer of needs, followers will move up to a new, higher-level set of needs.
4. Maslow's Hierarchy gives five broad categories of needs. It is up to Joe to fill in these categories with the unmet needs of his team. Understanding these needs gives Joe a path forward through this Rite of Passage and helps him *Respond to Followers' Changing Needs.*

Sagen's Mentoring Process:

1. Sagen worries Joe might have become too satisfied by his initial success, so he confronts the issue by asking whether their work together is done.
2. Sagen is pleased when Joe states he is not yet an extraordinary leader. Joe is prepared to do more work.
3. When Joe presents his revisions of Maslow's Hierarchy, Sagen gets to work, himself. He adds ten layers of follower needs which Joe had not seen.
4. Sagen reinforces the fact that once a lower-level set of needs is satisfied, followers will move up to higher-level sets of needs. He tells Joe his Rite of Passage here is to *Respond to Followers' Changing Needs*.
5. Sagen gives Joe an example of a leader who did not satisfy higher-level needs as they emerged (Mao) and one who did (Mandela).
6. Sagen tells Joe that transparent honesty is required from those below him in order for Joe to understand their present and changing needs.
7. Sagen reminds Joe, the recent moment in which his team was so transparent and so fully engaged may well have been temporary. It will be his leadership task to make this a permanent part of the company's culture.
8. He tells Joe that developing his own skill at detecting next-level needs is a difficult Rite of Passage, which he will be required to readdress many times during his career as he works to *Respond to Followers' Changing Needs*.

Case Study:

1. It took an entire year for this group of leaders to take the leap toward an adaptive strategy. Why? Was this organization suffering from complacency? If so, how can a group be in a state of pain and still be complacent?

2. Were group members not ready to take this responsibility one year earlier? Do you think they would have been ready at that time if there had been greater pain?

3. Were they all expecting Joe to address the problem on his own, or did this expectation solely come from Joe?

4. Was this one-year delay simply caused by the fact that Joe hadn't developed adequate leadership skills?

5. How has Joe changed during this year? If you believe he has changed, then is it fair to say he needed this time to mature before leading the present initiatives, or was the year away from Sagen just wasted time?

6. Is it believable that a firm like KC Miller Conveyor could be in the middle of a massive industry shift and its leaders not know it? Can you think of any well-known companies that failed to detect a shift in their industry?

7. In this chapter, the senior leadership team created a Hope Bearing Plan as a path to prosperity. Joe reports the entire climate of the firm improved subsequently, the mood is positive, and people are smiling and happy. Is this a believable outcome of simply establishing this plan? Why would some turnaround plans produce this result when others would not?

8. Is this positive mood just a honeymoon? What would make it sustainable?

9. Many leaders' greatest focus is on daily execution and they don't see themselves as in the business of *Responding to Followers' Changing Needs*. Is it valuable for them to see to themselves as *Responding to Followers' Changing Needs*? How would this benefit them and their organization?

10. Before reading the next chapter, please list some ways that Joe might understand and satisfy the changing needs of his followers.

11. What would be the first few steps he might take to begin the work of *Respond to Followers' Changing Needs*?

Chapter Eight

Eighth Rite of Passage: Transformational Leadership

It has been six months since Joe and Sagen last met. This time, however, the long timespan had been agreed upon. Soon after the last meeting, Joe phoned Sagen and said he had much leadership work to do and would return when he felt the need for a consultation.

Once again, Joe's first impression is that Sagen has aged noticeably in this brief period of time. However, he soon sees that Sagen remains impressively astute.

Joe begins, "I'm sure you could tell, in our last visit I was thrilled that my team had pulled together so nicely and had shared their insights and ideas. This allowed them to create a Hope Bearing Plan. The mood and climate in our workplace was quite positive. You warned me this might be a temporary state and suggested that I should look for ways to make it more permanent.

"I looked at the work you and I did on Maslow's chart and I remembered your words that my followers' needs, once met, will move up to a higher level, so I asked myself what needs I should focus on. I am working on two new initiatives. The first is to get the senior team to believe we can trust one another and to know we are safe among each other. This will allow us to speak openly, criticize new ideas, and improve processes without fear of repercussions.

"Regarding this first initiative, I spoke directly with our senior team about being open and sharing ideas without fear or hesitation. They all nodded their heads and agreed. However, I have not seen increased openness or trust in any of our subsequent conversations. I think perhaps they are not sure of my agenda and they are afraid they will run counter to my intentions. I must confess I bought the Des Moines acquisition single-handedly, with just a little help from the CFO. This history might have led them to conclude that I will continue to make secretive plans, which of course I will not."

"Could there be another reason?" Sagen asks.

"I wonder whether perhaps they just don't trust one another," Joe says.

"Joe, your instincts are good. Most likely, everything you have just described is in play. This should not be discouraging, however. It should simply show you where your leadership work is. If you are trying to get these people to be open with each other, to admit mistakes, and to engage in critical thinking together, you must do more than just ask them. You have to show them."

Sagen continues, "The process of building conveyor systems involves a complex sequence of steps and it includes many people. There are hundreds of momentary events every day. Orders come in and shipments go out. Some are on time and some are not. Some are accurate. Others are not. People collaborate. People fail to collaborate. From time to time there are billing mistakes. This goes on in every workplace. I recommend that in your senior team meetings you address some of these mistakes and look to see who had a hand in helping to create the mistake. It is always more than one person. For example, if finance is slow to get a bill out, it might mean sales was slow notifying warehouse, and warehouse was slow sending the ticket to finance. Your job is not to criticize those who have made mistakes. Rather, your job is to call the process."

Joe asks, "Call the process?"

"Yes, you are more interested in the processes behind mistakes than in blaming any one person. Coming to understand the process will require the entire team to establish open and frank honesty. It has been said that many people touch a mistake. Gaining an understanding of how all these people may have contributed to the problem is the goal. Let your team know you are doing this so they can become comfortable admitting mistakes and looking for solutions. You are looking at the process of how individuals, groups, and departments interact with each other. And Joe, be sure to include some mistakes of your own. This will show them you are vulnerable, and vulnerability is an important trait of an extraordinary leader."

"Okay, I can work on that."

Sagen says, "Eventually you and your team will want to do a root cause analysis, such as a Fishbone Diagram, on some of the problems but for now you are just trying to get these transparent conversations going. There are many resources that can teach you how to conduct a root cause analysis. It sounds more complicated than it is, really." [14]

Joe says, "Regarding a second initiative, I thought perhaps I could imitate some of the great leaders who spent time working side-by-side with their various follower-contingencies. I began this by having one-on-one conversations with each of my senior team members. I asked them to tell me what their greatest successes have been. As they described each one, I offered sincere praise. Then, I asked them to describe their greatest frustrations. Most of their frustrations seemed to be technical in nature, like supply chain and operational issues. Their answers were shallow.

"I then went to each department and frontline work group. I had small townhall meetings and made sure the supervisor or leader was present. I asked the same questions regarding their achievements and their frustrations. I also asked what we can do to make their work easier. I was surprised that they were much more open and eager to share their thoughts and ideas than was my senior team.

"I ended each townhall meeting by asking the employees if I could work with them, side-by-side, for three days. Of course, they were surprised by this. Some chuckled, and a few warehouse guys made comments telling me they didn't think I could handle it, but it was all good-natured."

Joe continues, "Some departments, such as warehouse, were easy for me. I enjoyed the physical labor and the high-energy of it. However, finance has its own complex systems for posting invoices and accounts receivable. I couldn't become fluent with this in just a few days, so they used me as a clerk and had me stuffing envelopes with bills, paychecks, and mail."

Sagen asks, "What was your motive?"

"My motive?"

"Yes."

"I wanted to connect with them, so I could become a beloved leader like Mandela or early Mao."

Sagen asserts, "That would be an outcome and it is not the right motive."

"Not the right motive? What would be the right motive?"

"We will get to that. First I must ask, what did you accomplish?"

Joe says, "I believe I created a better bond, a deeper connection, with my stakeholders."

Sagen is moving fast here as he asks, "And what did you learn?"

Joe repeats the question, "What did I learn? What did I learn?"

Joe looks down at the pad of paper on his lap and begins to scribble. Eventually he looks up but does not make eye contact with Sagen. Instead, he looks around the room. He scribbles again.

Joe speaks, "I learned a lot. We have some remarkably nice people working for us. There is something healthy and positive about them.

"However, I think we are not one big organization. Rather, we are a collection of islands. Inside those islands, a lot of people work hard, but I sense some animosity between departments and resistance toward each other. The finance department believes it is viewed to be unimportant and is not treated like a central part of the company. The warehouse is as chaotic and disorganized as Ron has told me.

"I learned more than that, Sagen. I learned that we do not have a corporate culture. Each department has its own way of doing things. Des Moines has one corporate personality and Kansas City has another. We do not have a unified strategy. Some of our work groups operate according to Relationship Platform, but others operate according to Efficient Platform. I have been preaching to them that we are both. It appears I have not succeeded at getting this message across."

Sagen interrupts, "Joe, you do have a corporate culture. You just described it. Unfortunately, it is not an adaptive culture that is cohesive and unified around your personal beliefs or the strategy you have chosen for your firm. It is loose, disconnected, and fragmented, but that is your culture at this moment."

Joe says, "Okay, that's a helpful insight. I also learned that some of our supervisors are kindly people and they are liked by their employees. Some are not. Beyond all that, I observed that a few of our employees are not fully engaged. They seem more interested in getting every minute out of their coffee break and lunch break than helping each other or serving the customer. These people do not go beyond the paycheck."

Sagen looks at Joe knowingly but does not speak. He breathes a long slow breath. This time it is he who looks around the room. He speaks:

"Joe, how do you plan to change this?"

Joe replies with a serious tone, "Sagen, I plan to scream and threaten them."

Sagen replies, "Well, that would be one approach."

"I'm kidding."

"I know."

Now Joe is sincere. "Perhaps you can give me a little guidance."

Sagen says, "Time to teach. Time to transform."

Joe asks, "Time for you to teach? Time for you to transform?"

"No, Joe. Time for you to do so."

Sagen says, "Now we can talk about what your motive should be. The motive for your gaining such deep contact with your team should be so you can learn which direction to move in, in order to transform your organization. It is time to transform.

"In his book, *Leadership,* James MacGregor Burns coins the phrase Transformational Leadership. He contrasts this with Transactional Leadership. Transactional Leadership is just what it sounds like; nothing more than a transaction. It seems you have some employees and managers who see their work as a simple transaction. They give you their hours and you give them money. Of course, this leads to a workforce that has a low level of engagement. [7]

"As you know, Joe, the mission you are traveling here is to *Create Followers.* Within that mission, your next Rite of Passage is *Transformational Leadership.* It requires the leader to engage followers on two levels. First, a leader must meet their needs. Second, he or she must gain the commitment of the entire group to pursue a higher-level purpose. Gaining this commitment to strive for a higher purpose almost always requires the leader to teach them about this purpose and to teach them what they will gain if the entire group can achieve the purpose.

"There is more to it than this. Transformational Leadership is complex. It is created as a product of a two-way dialogue between the leader and the followers. This dialogue further cements their relationship and creates stronger followership. The higher-level purpose that is chosen must meet three sets of needs: those of the leader, those of the followers, and those of the organization. And it must be for real. Any effort to falsely sell a purpose simply for the leader's gain will end in failure."

Joe has stopped writing. He is staring at Sagen.

Joe asks, "And if it works?"

"Joe, a shared purpose is powerful. Think about the many thousands of Chinese peasants who suffered and marched to their deaths behind Mao Zedong to fulfill their purpose. Think of the many who put their own lives at risk to follow Mandela so they could fulfill their purpose. This is why the shared purpose you choose must serve your followers, your company, and yourself."

Joe says, "But, we are not lifting peasants out of poverty and starvation. We are not ending the suffering of blacks in South Africa. We just make conveyors."

Sagen says, "To do the next element of work, we must move to the top of our Maslow chart. Do you recall I added the words, 'striving toward a higher purpose' at the top of your chart?"

Sagen builds his argument, "Mandela's followers were bound together by the purpose they shared. You must ask what purpose your entire company shares. And, you are correct, it's about more than just building conveyors. This speaks to what your motive should be; creating an organization where people are bound together by the purpose they share."

Joe repeats Sagen's words, "Bound together by the purpose they share."

They both allow a moment of silence to hang in the air.

Joe asks, "I know this is a little unusual, but can we take a break for 15 or 20 minutes?"

"Of course."

Joe goes outside and sits in a large wicker chair on the front porch while he sips some bottled water. He spends the first few minutes taking in the scenery and not working on these issues at all. Gradually, he begins to sort through each variable in the methodical way a good engineer would. He thinks of some solutions, works them, and then reworks them. He goes back inside.

"Sagen, I can see you are right. It all begins with creating a shared purpose. If we can collectively work toward the same goal, this will create enough forward-moving energy for us to define our mission, our future vision, and upon which to build our core values. It all begins with our selecting a shared purpose which will be powerful enough to bind us together."

Sagen says, "Once again I am quite impressed. Your insights are remarkable. Do you have an idea what this shared purpose will be?"

Joe speaks, "Well, we are not a pharmaceutical company whose purpose is to eradicate illness. Companies like that will find it easy to select a shared purpose. However, I constantly think about those days when our business almost failed and when we lost so many of our treasured colleagues. What we have today that was absent then is just one thing, prosperity. So, can generating prosperity be a firm's shared purpose?"

Sagen replies, "It can, but you should ask what the product of that prosperity is. I think your shared purpose lies somewhere in that realm. Joe, I want you to read a book, *Built to Last*, by Jim Collins and Jerry Porras. [15] This is another of my favorite leadership books. It talks about how our greatest companies did the very work you need to do. It has much to say about establishing core values and building a cult-like culture. It suggests you should build a culture so powerful that some people will be comfortable working for you, while others will not fit into the culture and will simply leave. There is a more recent Harvard Business Review article, titled 'The Power of Collective Ambition' that addresses this. I recommend it as well." [16]

Sagen asks, "As you do all this transformational work and as you attempt to build a cohesive culture, what is your real goal, Joe?"

"My real goal?"

Sagen does not reply.

"I guess I'm trying to build a team."

Again, no response from Sagen.

Joe says, "Okay, what I want to accomplish with this Rite of Passage is to create a work environment in which everyone has a sense of ownership, buys into our goals and methods, and loves each other and the business as much as I do. You once asked me if I am *All In*. I am trying to create a work environment in which everybody is *All In*."

Joe asks, "May I have a few months to work on this? I can see my challenge here is to teach my senior team about this, and through this teaching we should select a shared purpose that will allow us to move my organization up to a higher-level. Actually, I don't want to simply move my organization to this higher-level. I want to transform it. It makes sense that this Rite of Passage is called, *Transformational Leadership*."

"Take all the time you need, Joe. Remember, the name of this overall mission is *Create Followers*. To succeed at this, you must master *Transformational Leadership*. Gaining this competency is an important Rite of Passage on your journey toward becoming an extraordinary leader."

Joe's Rite of Passage:

1. Joe begins actively attempting to select and meet the new higher-level needs of his followers.

2. In order to transform his senior team, Joe simply instructs them to become more open and to share ideas without fear or hesitation. He is surprised when this transformation does not happen simply because he says it should.

3. Joe establishes stakeholder listening sessions. He starts with his senior team, and then he goes out to the field. He finds hourly workers to be more open and self-disclosing than his senior team.

4. Joe offers to work side-by-side with people in the various departments.

5. Joe observes and learns much about his organization. He sees that his culture is fragmented because things are done differently in each location. There is no uniform posture regarding how managers will treat employees and how employees will conduct business.

6. After listening to Sagen, Joe begins to understand that creating a shared purpose will be the foundation upon which his team builds its mission, future vision, and core values. He quotes Sagen, "Bound together by the purpose they share." This is the basis of *Transformational Leadership.*

7. Developing his ability to generate *Transformational Leadership* is Joe's next Rite of Passage.

Sagen's Mentoring Process:

1. Sagen allows a long absence again. He knows the pace of leadership development will depend on the abilities of the aspiring leader and this might not be the pace the mentor desires.
2. Sagen teaches Joe that if he wants higher-level functioning in his senior team, he must show them and not simply tell them.
3. Sagen teaches Joe how to call the process. This gives the group permission to examine the processes they use to interact with one another and to objectively examine the root causes of mistakes and problems.
4. Regarding Joe's listening sessions and his campaign of working side-by-side, Sagen makes Joe do some work. He questions his motive, what he accomplished, and what he learned.
5. When Joe sees that his culture is so fragmented, Sagen teaches him about *Transformational Leadership*. He tells Joe it is based on a two-way dialogue and must truly meet the needs of the organization, leader, and followers.
6. Sagen says that the way to begin a transformation is by creating a shared purpose within the organization.
7. Sagen does not tell Joe directly that Joe desires a team in which everyone is *All In*. Rather, he probes with open-ended questions until Joe announces this.
8. Sagen is pleased with Joe's grasp of *Transformational Leadership*. He looks forward to the next visit.

Case Study:

1. Why would senior leadership team members ever want to be open and vulnerable with one another? Isn't it in their best interest to be guarded and self-protective? Is there a real advantage to the organization if this trust and vulnerability is established?

2. Sagen encourages Joe to show his own vulnerability by admitting mistakes. Is this really a good idea? What are the downside risks of Joe doing this?

3. Should Joe persistently and gradually try to improve the ways senior team members interact with one another or should he simply demand it?

4. What does Sagen mean by "call the process"?

5. Joe goes down into the front lines of the organization and sees various cells that function quite differently from each other. There are some supervisors who are nice and some who are not. There are some work groups which are effective and some which are not. How could this have developed?

6. Joe says he doesn't have a culture but Sagen says this is incorrect, adding that what Joe observes is Joe's culture. He has a culture which is fragmented, disjointed, and lacking in unity. Who is right here, Joe or Sagen? Can a firm have no culture?

7. Sagen uses the phrase "cult-like culture". Do you like this phrase? Please explain why or why not. What companies do you know that have cult-like cultures? In those companies, is the culture only internal or does it relate also to the firm's customer-facing activities? How?

8. Are cult-like cultures always positive, or can there be a nasty or negative cult-like culture?

9. Sagen recommends creating a shared purpose. He seems to believe this is a powerfully motivating force, if done right. Do you agree? Do you know of an organization in which there is a shared purpose, but the organization is still quite dysfunctional? If so, what causes that organization to be dysfunctional? So, can it be said that establishing a shared purpose within an organization is necessary and sufficient to create a unified and motivated culture? Or, is it necessary but not sufficient? If you say it is not sufficient, what else would be needed?

10. Sagen tells Joe it is time to teach and transform. He introduces the concept of *Transformational Leadership* in which a leader substantially changes the nature of an organization. Can you name some political leaders (other than Mao and Mandela) who have succeeded at *Transformational Leadership*? Please describe how they shifted their civic or national culture from what it was before to what it became after the transformation.

Chapter Nine

Ninth Rite of Passage: Get Them All to Be All In

Once again Joe is warmly greeted by Sagen. After taking his seat, Joe hands Sagen a small package.

Sagen lifts out a beautiful rectangular box and opens it, "These look exquisite. May I ask what they are?"

Joe answers, "Fleur de sel soft caramel chocolates. Making chocolates from scratch is one of my wife's hobbies. She asked me to bring these today."

Sagen says, "Please tell her thank you. I am quite impressed. We must have some now. Can I get you some coffee to go with these beautiful treats?"

"Yes, please."

Sagen hands Joe a cup of coffee. Joe takes a sip and asks, "Ethiopian?"

Starbucks®.

They both chuckle.

A moment later Sagen prompts, "So, please tell all."

Joe begins, "We asked an industrial psychologist to work with us, and we stayed with him for several months. He reminds me of you, Sagen. He asks probing questions and makes the group work to get the answers. He knows a lot about competitive models, mission statements, and core values.

"We began with our purpose and I suggested that generating prosperity would be an admirable shared purpose. He asked what was admirable about it, so I told our story about how this company nearly closed its doors, and how many good people suffered. I told him if I can ensure this will never happen again, I will consider myself to have been a good leader. Of course, he asked why prosperity is important.

"I told him now we have over 200 employees in three states and this means 700 pairs of school shoes every August, 600 to 800 doctor visits per year, and 200 turkeys on Thanksgiving tables.

"He asked why these things are important.

"This question got our entire senior team all talking at the same time, as if he had asked the most ridiculous question. They said these are the things that give us and our families a good life. Without them we will suffer, and so will our children.

"He then asked who else benefits from this prosperity. Again, answers came from everyone on our team, but their point was that we generate prosperity for one another, the company, our vendors, and our customers. If KC Miller Conveyor is successful, prosperity travels through a long line of beneficiaries. This helps them and their families to have a good life."

Joe continues, "Based on this, we decided that our shared purpose is to help bring a good life to one another, our vendors, and our customers.

"Please notice that we said, 'help bring a good life' and, the word 'help' is important here. We don't guarantee a good life, but we can do a lot that allows a person to have a good life. This includes a good life at work, along with the benefits that flow from prosperity into the home and family."

Sagen asks, "What requirement does this place on your teammates?"

Joe says, "This idea of helping to bring a good life to our employees creates a higher-level requirement that we must treat employees well, be courteous, and have an emotionally healthy work environment. I don't believe we have emphasized these things enough, and certainly not in a uniform way across the entire organization."

"Very good, Joe. Very good. What about other things like a mission, future vision, and core values?"

"Our consultant worked with us on these topics as well. As our sessions with him progressed, I began writing these things on a whiteboard in my office using a dry-erase marker. I told the leadership team that when we are done with all this, we must take it out to groups of employees. Rather than present it to them, we should ask some of the same questions. We should listen carefully to them, and then later we can announce our purpose, mission, future vision, and core values. During the subsequent two months, all members of our senior team went out in teams of two to every workgroup to all three states where our employees work. They asked our employees what our purpose, mission and core values should be."

Sagen says, "Well done. The dry-erase marker interests me."

"I wanted the senior team to know that we were working to create a rough draft of these important concepts, but this work will be of little value without the support of everyone."

Sagen says, "That which is imposed is rarely embraced."

Joe hands Sagen a chart.

The KC Miller Way

Shared Purpose:
We help bring a good life to one another, our vendors, and our customers.

How we fulfill our shared purpose:
1.   We gladly take on a shared responsibility to make the whole business succeed.
2.   We care about each other, help one another get the work done, and offer support when one of our own undergoes a personal crisis.
3.   We work to create prosperity for ourselves, each other, our company, our vendors, and our customers.

Mission:
We make it easy for our customers to operate ever-more efficiently and grow their business.

How we fulfill our mission:
1.   We are hassle-free and on time with the right order, and accurate billing. And we are cooperative.
2.   We teach our vendors about our customers' needs. This allows us to give customers exactly what they need.

Future Vision:
Within five years, KC Miller Conveyor will be the most highly trusted supplier of conveyor systems in the 13 states that make up the middle of America.

How we will fulfill our future vison:
1.   By acquisitions.
2.   Organically, by increasing our sales force.
3.   By building a hub and spoke model with large warehouses in the center surrounded by small depots.
4.   By having one central dispatch office which will route trucks and manage the entire distribution process.

Core Values:
1.   We build deep relationships based on honesty, integrity, and trust.
2.   We are willing to work through the night to help a customer solve a problem.
3.   We operate as a team.
4.   We are on time and accurate.
5.   We all work to improve processes and outcomes for ourselves, our customers, and our vendors.

Joe is not surprised that Sagen takes his time and studies this chart carefully.

Sagen says, "Once again I am highly impressed with your work."

"Thank you."

Sagen allows a long silence and then says, "Very good, Joe. Very good. The shared purpose of helping to bring a good life matches your firm very well. Your mission of making things easy for your customers nicely matches your dual Relationship and Efficient Platforms."

Sagen resumes his work, "I do have a few questions for you. Is there a reason you did not elaborate on how you will fulfill your core values? You did so in all the other categories."

Joe replies, "We attempt to fulfill our core values in all we do, every day. That list would be too long. The core values will need to stand on their own."

Sagen says, "I agree."

Sagen asks, "Did you get a chance to read *Built to Last*, and the article on collective ambition?"

Joe states he has read them both.

Sagen says, "As I would have expected from you."

Sagen asks, "Your future vision is quite ambitious. Is this simply your vision or is it a collective ambition?"

Joe says, "We did something that went beyond any advice we were given. At first, we thought simply getting the input from all employees would have been enough effort to allow them to feel included and for them to experience a sense of ownership of all this. Our employees gave us excellent guidance when we first asked them to help us create The KC Miller Way. They participated enthusiastically. After each session many of them came up and shook our hands. Several said they knew they were participating in something big.

"After doing all this, we did something extreme. After the initial round of listening sessions, our senior team constructed The KC Miller Way in my office. This was heavily influenced by the input we had received from all directions. Then we went back out to the field and we presented it to all employees. We asked if we had heard them accurately and whether this represented their view. Their reaction was passionate, and their passion truly touched my heart.

"This experience pulled together many of the lessons you have taught me. Just like Nelson Mandela, I looked at this from the employees' point of view. Your lesson on *Transformational Leadership* influenced me greatly. In the sessions before we finalized The KC Miller Way, we sought input, but we also spent a good deal of time teaching.

"Sagen, in our follow-up visits I asked each group how this will benefit them. Their answers were spot-on. They openly talked about building a better team, outpacing the competition, and creating prosperity which would benefit us all, our families, our vendors, and our customers. As of now, I believe there has been a transformation. My team and I will work to maintain this transformation as we go into the future."

Sagen instructs, "Joe, it is not enough to simply have a great shared purpose, mission statement, future vision, and core values. You are already fully engaged with your next Rite of Passage, which is to *Get Them All to Be All In*. To accomplish this, you must operationalize all these things. In the first moments of every meeting, I encourage you to ask for an example of how someone has executed your mission, an example of how they have fulfilled your purpose, and perhaps an example of how someone has displayed a core value. You can do this gently. It does not need to seem like a quiz. This should all be done by your subordinate leaders as well. Your onboarding process for new employees must be centered around The KC Miller Way. That is where you will begin to indoctrinate them into your culture. That is where you will show them what *All In* means. Your annual performance reviews should also be built on The KC Miller Way. As you move about in the company you should stop an employee and congratulate him or her for doing something that fits within The KC Miller Way. You should have award ceremonies in the same manner. Your big challenge is to integrate, promote, and preach The KC Miller Way in a constant and ongoing manner. You are trying to build a cult-like culture."

Sagen says, "Joe, all of this is intended to *Get Them All to Be All In*. That is your Rite of Passage now."

"Again, Sagen, I say thank you for all of this. Thank you very much."

"You are welcome, Joe."

Joe's Rite of Passage:

1. Joe sees that *Get Them All to Be All In* begins with finding a collective purpose that will engage his entire workforce. In this case, it is about more than generating profits. It is about helping to bring a good life to a long line of beneficiaries.

2. Joe and his team accurately create The KC Miller Way by aligning the collective purpose with the company's mission, future vision, and core values.

3. During the process of creating The KC Miller Way, Joe wages a campaign to seek input from all stakeholders. He hopes this effort will give them a sense of ownership. Once The KC Miller Way is created, Joe takes it out to them again to ensure it meets their needs and to strengthen their sense of ownership.

4. Joe will teach and preach The KC Miller Way in every circumstance he can.

5. Joe is moving nicely through this Rite of Passage. He is building a culture. He is working to *Create Followers* and to *Get Them All to Be All In*. He will get his subordinate leaders to do so, too.

Sagen's Mentoring Process:

1. Sagen observes that his relationship with Joe has continued to become more personal. Joe brings him specialty chocolates. This is more than just a gift. It represents that Joe views himself as becoming Sagen's colleague.

2. Having engaged a local organizational psychologist, Joe works with him without first seeking Sagen's guidance. Sagen is pleased with this because it shows that Joe is becoming less dependent on him. Joe is more competent and more confident. Sagen observes that Joe's journey toward extraordinary leadership has become more self-sustained now.

3. Sagen knows why Joe uses the dry-erase marker, but he asks him to explain anyway, thus forcing Joe to work his way through his own logic.

4. Sagen praises Joe for returning to each stakeholder group by saying simply, "That which is imposed is rarely embraced."

5. Toward the end of their session Joe has said nothing about executing The KC Miller Way throughout all levels of the company, so Sagen instructs him on how to do this. He suggests Joe and all his leaders could open meetings by asking for a core value, and other similar steps. He implies these efforts will *Get Them All to Be All In*.

Case Study:

1. Joe begins this visit by bringing Sagen a gift, exotic chocolates. Is it appropriate for Joe to give Sagen a gift? Does this say something about their relationship?

2. What would have been the implications of this gift if it had been given in Joe's first or second session?

3. Joe pays Sagen an indirect compliment when he describes the consultant, "He reminds me of you, Sagen. He asks probing questions and makes the group work to get the answers." What is the significance of this compliment?

4. Please comment on the process Joe used in creating The KC Miller Way. He put great time and effort into it. Do most CEOs or leaders put this much time into this type of project? Aren't they too busy?

5. After creating The KC Miller Way, Joe takes it out to the employees and seeks their input. Is this extra step commonly done? Have you seen it done? Would you do it if you were in Joe's place?

6. Please note that Sagen does not edit The KC Miller Way as he had done with Joe's efforts with Maslow's Hierarchy of Needs. How do you make sense of this?

7. Do you work in a firm that either does not have a well-defined or highly promoted "Way"? Perhaps it has core values on a poster in the breakroom, but most people don't know what they are. Could you establish purpose, mission, vision, and values for your own team or department? How would you align them with the larger organization?

8. Joe has said his firm is simultaneously built on a Relationship Platform and an Efficient Platform. However, his mission statement only points to helping customers build efficiencies. In his industry, how would building customer efficiencies also strengthen the firm's Relationship Platform?

Third Mission: Become a Leader of Leaders

The Four Passages of the Third Mission: Become a Leader of Leaders

10. Hand it Over

11. Become a Leader of Leaders

12. Make Them Partners

13. Empower Your Leaders to Build Their Teams

Chapter Ten

Tenth Rite of Passage: Hand It Over

More than a decade has passed since Joe and his team created The KC Miller Way. During this time, Joe's sessions with Sagen have become infrequent but still treasured. Sometimes six months to a year can pass between visits. Today, Joe sits in the same chair he sat in when he was 25 years old. Sagen appears further diminished by age. By comparison Joe seems to radiate incrementally more poise and confidence.

Joe begins, "You know, Sagen, most people think of Colorado as a winter place, but it was 97 degrees when I left Kansas City today and this cool mountain air is refreshing."

Sagen replies, "Not just good for the lungs. Good for the soul."

"For sure," says Joe.

Sagen asks, "Joe, will you please describe your latest innovations?"

Joe says, "When I first met you, computers existed only in very large companies and universities. Today we have our own PCs and servers. In those days there was no Internet. I know the Internet is new, but I have great hope for what it will do for us eventually.

"With the help of some programmers, we have automated our shipping processes in the warehouse and tied this to our finance department so everything that gets shipped out automatically generates its own invoice. We have written a program that keeps track of the volumes of everything each supplier delivers to us. This program also tells us the list of parts which go into every conveyor system we sell to each customer. This is important because some parts can go into several different conveyor systems. In order for it to work right, this software requires every department to work as a team with every other department.

"All of this strengthens our two competitive platforms. Of course, by this I mean our Efficient Platform and our Relationship Platform."

Sagen asks, "I see how it would strengthen your Efficient Platform, but can you please explain how it strengthens your Relationship Platform?"

"Well, we believe the Relationship Platform requires us to have deep knowledge of our customers and this knowledge gives us ways to meet each customer's needs. We keep track of every conveyor system our customers buy and we can see patterns. We can tell them what parts they need to replace before they are aware of it, so no customer's conveyor goes down. As we have become more efficient, we have been able to gradually lower our prices. This has been extremely pleasing to our customers. All of this allows our customers to be much more successful. Our improved efficiencies increase our customers' attachment to us and this deepens our relationship."

Sagen asks, "This computer programming you talk about gives you a great strategic advantage, but aren't you worried that your competitors could create the same software?"

"We have thought about that and decided it's not just the software. It is also our skill at tying this software to The KC Miller Way that gives us our advantage. No competitor could fully execute The KC Miller Way or make it interface with this software the way we can."

Sagen says, "Very interesting."

Sagen continues, "You have been on a long leadership journey since we first met. You have successfully traveled through many Rites of Passage. You are a remarkable leader."

Joe smiles and asks, "An extraordinary leader?"

Sagen has begun his work already. "What do you think about that, Joe?"

"When we first met, I was focused only on external circumstances and events. Thanks to you, Sagen, I began examining my own leadership development many years ago. Fully developing my leadership abilities has become my life's work. I can't say I'm an extraordinary leader at this time. Somehow, I don't believe I have crossed that finish line. Perhaps no one ever does. If I were an extraordinary leader, I would not carry some of the frustrations that I carry with me with me every day."

"Tell me about these frustrations."

"Actually, I am eager to tell you about this. You see, leadership can be lonely for me at times. Truly, I don't have anyone at work with whom I can really talk about my frustrations and burdens. Maybe that's how it should be. I am the CEO and so I need to appear confident. I appreciate being able to talk with you about these things."

Sagen listens.

"I have a great team. Everyone who works for me is *All In*. They understand The KC Miller Way. It would seem I have no reason to feel dissatisfied. But some days I go home exhausted, and on those days, I am frustrated that there are so many tasks I haven't had time to address."

Sagen asks, "You have created strong followership, yes?"

"Yes."

"How large is your organization now, Joe?"

"We have 1,700 employees and we serve 15 states."

"How much time do you spend traveling to these locations? And, what do you do when you get to them?"

"Typically, I am on the road four days each week. At every location I examine their P&L, customer lists, order patterns, cash flow, aging of accounts receivable, and operational issues. I always make a good effort to pay a compliment to the department I am reviewing and I make sure to praise someone for executing The KC Miller Way. Then we look at how any problems can be resolved. When I return to that location, usually a month later, I make sure to ask about any progress that has been made."

Sagen interrupts, "So far, this sounds like normal supervisory visits. Where does the frustration come from?"

Joe replies, "There are two sources of my frustration. First, I can't get it all done. All this travel time takes me away from my office. I bring work with me on the road and do it in the evenings. I also put in more hours than I should on Saturday and Sunday just to catch up, but I never do get caught up.

"I have a second frustration as well. If I look at our overall company revenues, I see increasing numbers quarter over quarter and year over year. However, a closer look reveals that all that revenue growth is occurring in our original three locations. In the other locations, our gross revenues are flat or declining. Initially there was some mystery to this because our sales team is landing an impressive number of new accounts in those outlying areas, so one would expect to see increasing revenues from each location. It turns out that acquiring new accounts isn't the problem. Keeping existing accounts is the problem.

"We now cast a wide geographic net, and our accounts in the outlying areas are being stolen by large and small competitors who pick them off one by one."

Sagen replies with empathy, "Even as you describe this, I detect your worry and your deep sense of disappointment."

"Yes, I would say I am disappointed in myself because I'm not sure what else I can do. I am now a seasoned leader. I have created a strong following. Our firm has a compelling purpose and clear core values. And we have a well-defined competitive platform. All of this should lead us to success."

Sagen says, "Perhaps we might look at this through a different lens. Please allow me to ask you a few questions. What impression do new employees get when they are hired by your firm?"

Joe replies, "I hope they get a positive impression. I hope they see us as competent, caring, and well regarded in our industry. That's the impression we hope to give them."

Sagen says, "You haven't said anything about fostering a sense of worry or anxiety in the new employee. Perhaps they don't see the same need to perform that your teammates in the first three locations see. Perhaps they see a solid company which will be around for 100 years, will pay them well, and escort them into a comfortable retirement."

"Perhaps so."

Sagen says, "Joe, we call this complacency. Do you remember something you and I talked about long ago? You told me a military officer must always know his location, where he is. The developmental location of your company now could best be called steady-state. That is a nice place to be, but the danger of being a successful incumbent in your industry is that the employee may begin to develop a posture of complacency. There is a wonderful book on how to overcome complacency by Judith Bardwick, titled *Danger in the Comfort Zone.*[17] I recommend you read it.

"Maybe you should do what Andy Grove does over at Intel. He has built a successful enterprise, but each day he asks himself what he would do with the company if today were his first day as the new CEO. It seems you must ask yourself some hard questions, like whether some of your leaders in the outlying areas are competent. Perhaps you should ask whether you have replicated your original culture in those locations. All these problems tend to exist in successful companies that are in the stage that we call steady-state. This steady-state breeds complacency and complacency must be disrupted."

Sagen continues, "So, as I describe all of this, does it sound the trumpet that marches you into battle to solve these problems?"

Joe replies, "Yes it does. You know me well."

"Joe, it is clear that there are a few more Rites of Passage calling to you. The problem is that you still see yourself as the leader. Do you remember long ago I told you I would send you on four missions and within each mission there would be multiple Rites of Passage?"

"Of course. I remember it well."

"You are beginning your third mission, *Become a Leader of Leaders.*"

Joe is quiet for a moment. *"Become a Leader of Leaders?* Are you going to tell me how I would accomplish this?"

Sagen does not answer.

"So, once again you want me to answer my own question?"

Again, no answer from Sagen.

A moment later Joe says, "It sounds like I am taking too much on my own shoulders, just as I have done so many times before."

Sagen instructs, "Your organization is now too complex for you to be the only real leader. Until now you have had your hands on everything. From this point forward, you need to use the hands of others. It is expecting too much for one person to lead all aspects of this business, and if you try to do so you will fall short. Trying harder, yourself, will not bring you any closer to success. This is a common point of failure in organizational development. The inability to move from an entrepreneurial posture to a posture of leading through others has caused many great leaders to fall. From this point forward, you should define your leadership as getting your work done through others."

Joe echoes, "Leadership now is getting my work done through others."

Sagen replies, "Lead. Don't do. Again, your new mission is *Become a Leader of Leaders.* There are four Rites of Passage within this mission. The name of the first of these four Rites of Passage is *Hand It Over."*

Sagen says, "Think of your own leadership journey. You have traveled through many passages. Now it will be your job to mentor others through their leadership passages in a similar way as I have mentored you. You are no longer in the business of running your business. You are in the business of getting others to run your business. Your connection to the business is through them."

"I know there is truth to what you are saying," Joe says, "but I have always thought of myself as a supportive leader who does encourage others to succeed and do well. It is difficult for me to see how I have failed to lead through others."

"Joe, I believe you have done so in your inner circle, with those who are close to you. However, now you must do so with a much broader segment of your organization. Do you remember when I first suggested your team *Enter the Cone of Uncertainty*? The intent there was to place more of the anxiety and responsibility on those around you and remove some of it from yourself. This is similar. Here I am suggesting that you hand these responsibilities to vice presidents, sales managers, depot managers, and others. Your followers' reactions will be very similar to when you asked your small group to *Enter the Cone of Uncertainty*. Just like them, these followers will resist accepting this responsibility, but once they do accept this responsibility, you will have multiplied your leadership influence. This is why this Rite of Passage is called *Hand It Over.*"

Joe repeats, "*Hand It Over.*"

Sagen says, "Yes, *Hand It Over*. All of it. Make them responsible to understand what the problems are, come up with solutions, and execute plans. Make them work with each other. Encourage them to fully engage their own groups of employees. Cause them to energize and engage their people around the same collective purpose that you have been promoting. Require them to measure processes and outcomes. Make them leaders. Of course, you will be involved and you should know their plans, but you should not solve their problems for them. Hand them the anxiety and the responsibility."

Joe responds, "I see what you are saying, but I don't see how this reduces turnover in our new accounts."

Sagen says, "When you go out to the field, you are shown instances where your people in the outlying areas have competently executed The KC Miller Way. You acknowledge this to your teammates in those locations. However, they do not show you those moments when The KC Miller Way goes unexecuted or is executed in a mediocre manner. If you are losing new accounts in those environments, it is most likely that they are not competing out there the same way your teams do in your three legacy locations. They are not perfectly executing your competitive platforms. You are too far removed, geographically, for you to do this work for them. You must *Hand It Over* to them, coach them, and help them execute those things that give your firm its unique competitive advantage and its remarkable culture."

Joe replies, "This will be an extremely difficult Rite of Passage for me. As you know so well, I give my whole self to this business every day. This will feel like I am holding back and not giving it my all. It will be quite uncomfortable for me at first."

Sagen says, "Yes, that very sentiment is the reason so few entrepreneurs can move from being company builders to company leaders, and fewer still become extraordinary leaders. Your mission now is to *Become a Leader of Leaders*. Your first Rite of Passage within this mission is to *Hand It Over*. If you can accomplish this, you will have learned how to lead by using the talents and energies of others."

Joe's Rite of Passage:

1. Joe is an effective leader already. We see he has created custom-made inventory tracking and supply chain software that requires multiple individuals and departments to act in concert with each other. He passes the benefits of this to his customers. It appears that Joe is on top of his game.

2. However, Joe is frustrated. He trusts his relationship with Sagen, so he tells him about his frustrations.

3. Joe continues to study his own leadership development. He tells Sagen that when they first met, he was externally focused but now he has shifted his focus toward examining himself and his leadership skills. This has become a lifelong journey.

4. Like most leaders whose firms move from small to large, Joe still believes he can accomplish anything if he generates heroic personal effort. Despite this, he senses that he is failing in some way.

5. At first, Joe sees Sagen's suggestions that he *Hand It Over* and lead through others as recommendations that he should not be *All In*. His initial response is to offer resistance to this idea.

6. After this momentary resistance, Joe accepts this Rite of Passage. He must *Hand It Over*.

Sagen's Mentoring Process:

1. Sagen senses the high level of trust between Joe and him. Joe is willing to share things with Sagen that he, as CEO, cannot share with his closest teammates.

2. As Joe discloses more, Sagen offers him some sincere empathy. He can see Joe is trying his best but that Joe is experiencing real frustration. Sagen probes a little deeper into Joe's emotions by using the word, "disappointment".

3. Sagen knows this Rite of Passage well because almost all leaders whose organizations have moved from small to large will experience this same set of frustrations. These interventions come easily to Sagen, but the work is not easy for Joe.

4. Sagen proposes that trying harder will not bring Joe any closer to success. Now he must use the talents of others to get his work done.

5. Sagen exposes this Rite of Passage by telling Joe to stop being the sole leader and start to *Become a Leader of Leaders*.

6. To continue his journey toward becoming an extraordinary leader, Sagen tells Joe this Rite of Passage requires that he *Hand It Over*.

Case Study:

1. Joe, now mid-career, has expanded to 15 states, and has 1,700 employees. His team has created a homemade version of supply chain software long before it became commercially available. He is strengthening his competitive platforms. Shouldn't all this qualify him as an extraordinary leader? Please make the case, pro and con.

2. In addition to the above, Joe tells Sagen he has developed strong followership. Most certainly, his employees like him. Shouldn't this be enough to call him an extraordinary leader?

3. It sounds as if Joe is working 70-hour weeks. Isn't this typical of a leader with his level of responsibilities?

4. Sagen gives Joe little guidance about how to *Hand It Over*. Please describe the specific steps Joe would take to do this.

5. In order to *Hand It Over*, should Joe decline to answer his followers' questions when they encounter strategic or operational issues? Would this force them to make decisions and take responsibility?

6. Does *Hand It Over* mean Joe would simply manage by measuring outcomes? If so, which outcomes would they be?

7. Sagen suggests that the KC Miller culture is not being well executed in the outlying areas. How can Joe *Hand It Over* and still develop a well-executed culture there?

8. If you were in Joe's situation, would you resist Sagen's instructions to *Hand It Over*? Why or why not? How easy or difficult would this be for you?

Chapter Eleven

Eleventh Rite of Passage: Become a Leader of Leaders

It has been only one month since Joe's last visit. This time Joe offers no pleasantries about the beautiful mountains. It is early autumn and the sky is overcast, rendering a cold steady drizzle.

Sagen begins the interview, "Joe, do you remember long ago we talked about how as each level of need is met, a new and elevated level of need emerges?"

"I remember it well."

Sagen asks, "How has this been going for you?"

Joe replies, "Of course, when I first tackled the issue of meeting followers' needs so long ago, I shared this concept with my senior team. We have focused on many sets of needs over the years. As time has passed, each new set of needs has been progressively harder to detect. The most sophisticated needs tend to hide in the shadows of our day-to-day work. Overall, I think we've done a good job on this, but not a great job. However, there is one layer of need that we have not been able to address. Maslow called it esteem. We give out awards and mark the anniversaries of our people but somehow, we are falling short on this one. Considering the success we all have achieved at KC Miller Conveyor, I would think my front-line managers should be a little more self-assured and perhaps carry a more visible sense of pride."

Sagen says, "Ah, yes. Really, we are talking about self-esteem. When you ran cross-country in high school, your coach taught you how to be a long-distance runner by pacing yourself, using breathing techniques, and managing your posture as you ran. When you performed well in a race, you knew you had really achieved something. Others can teach you, but no one can run the race for you. Your coach never told you he would run the second and third mile for you so you could perform better. Only you were out there to perform well or poorly, on your own. Therefore, as you generated one good performance after another, your self-confidence went up. So did your self-esteem as well as your own sense of personal pride.

"The problem now is that you have been doing the work of your vice presidents and directors. You have been running their race for them. This has given them little opportunity to develop self-confidence and personal pride. Even now, as you work diligently to hand over tasks to them, you do not sense an increase in their self-esteem. Is that correct?"

"Yes, I believe that's correct."

Sagen asks, "Is it possible that many of them are eager to lead but don't really know how to do so? Could your history of having done their work for them have left them inexperienced?"

"I suppose this is quite possible in some cases."

Sagen says, "There is no reason to be discouraged. This simply instructs us about the work you are being called to do here."

Joe says, "Yes, this is where the work is. I want them to have the same sense of personal pride and passion that I have for this enterprise."

Sagen asks, "Can you please tell me why you want this?"

"I want them to have this passion because I need stakeholders. I want them to make a personal investment and to display this investment through their leadership, but I don't know how to operationalize this. Is there some type of step-by-step sequence?"

Sagen answers, "Your Rite of Passage here has the same name as this mission, to *Become a Leader of Leaders*. Begin by attending the meetings they run. Observe. And, as you do this, bear in mind, each of these leaders will be at his or her own unique level of leadership development. Some will be quite capable and so you can move into higher-level work with them. Others will struggle with the basics."

Joe says, "I have been attending a few of their meetings from time to time and you are right, each leader is different. Several seem to have natural leadership talent. I would rate them as competent, but still having some work to do. And then there are others who concern me. One man, Ron Graeber, has no structure to his meetings. They are just rambling discussions during which the topics of conversation spiderweb all over the place and at the end of the meeting there are no takeaways. On the other hand, Scott Larson is a bull. When he runs a meeting, it is clear that the outcome of the meeting has been decided by him in advance. He overpowers even the mildest attempt to engage in critical thinking about any issue."

Sagen says, "This Rite of Passage requires work on two levels. First, there is the work that you must do to further relinquish some of your tasks and hand them over to subordinates. You have said this is difficult for you. This will require you to actively coach and mentor these people in order to help them build their leadership skills. So, that's the first level. The second level is work that they must do. They will not become competent leaders simply because you coach them. In order for this to succeed, they must be receptive to the task and to your coaching. They need to take their own leadership development on as their life's work, just as you have done with yourself.

"It might be a good idea for you to begin in the beginning with some of these people. There is a difference between leadership and basic supervision. Sometimes we expect people to be competent leaders, but we haven't trained them how to be competent front-line supervisors. Front-line supervisory skills come first. There are many ways to do this. They could have monthly lunch-and-learn meetings in their own shops and work their way through a supervisory textbook.

Edwin Leonard and Kelly Trusey have written a great book on this, titled *Supervision: Concepts and Practices of Management*." [18]

Sagen continues, "There is another book that bridges the gap between supervision and leadership, titled *The Four Disciplines of Execution*. [19] One concept that pertains here is that each of your leaders should keep score. One of the authors, Chris McChesney, offers a good video presentation. [20] He talks about what it's like for teenage boys to be shooting the basketball without keeping score. They are relaxed and perform poorly. McChesney states that they become increasingly engaged and their performance improves once they start keeping score. For your people, keeping score will allow them to measure their performance and develop pride and self-esteem as their performance and the performance of their team improves."

Joe says, "Sagen you have said I should mentor them the way you have mentored me. However, I don't see myself in some of them."

Sagen replies, "As you travel through this Rite of Passage to *Become a Leader of Leaders*, your greatest leadership challenge is to accept the differences in each of these individuals. These people are not you. Each has his or her own unique history, style, and personality. Overall, you need to let them be who they are. Let them sing with their own voices and in their own authentic way. As you work with them, try to get them to self-observe their reflexive emotional habits and to move beyond the limits of some of those habits.

"Try to recall that one of your reflexive habits early on was to attempt to make all the decisions yourself. At first, this habit served you well. Eventually it got in your way. So it will be with each of them. Each will have his or her own reflexive habits, and those habits will have served them well. It is up to you to work with them to see the ways those habits have become self-limiting."

Sagen instructs, "This Rite of Passage calls you to *Become a Leader of Leaders*. Please recall, in our last visit I said leadership for you now is getting your work done through others. You are now in the business of coaching. In doing this you are attempting to build basic leadership skills in your key people. Get them to identify themselves as leaders. Ask them to *Take the Lead* just as you did.

Teach them that the initiatives they launch are in fact theirs and that they are not doing things just because the boss says so.

"Early on, encourage them to address a Technical Leadership challenge with their work teams. This would be a task that they already have the skills to execute, but it might seem difficult to them. Prompt them to call their employees into action, to lead, facilitate, and encourage. As you observe this process occurring, you will see the various places where it will stall. Try to resist advising your leaders beforehand about how they might avoid these pitfalls. Let them become frustrated with the actions and inactions of their people. Let your leaders go through this. All these struggles are good opportunities for you to coach them afterward."

Joe asks, "I think I have a few who can succeed at all of this now. What direction do I go with them?"

Sagen replies, "Pre-coach them that they should present an Adaptive Leadership challenge to their team. Of course, this means they should ask the group to do something it doesn't know how to do. Usually this is something big. Watch how they handle the interactions between their employees. Observe how they seek input, whether they include the silent ones, and whether they are able to get the group to engage in critical thinking and to create new perspectives. All of this is rich opportunity for you to coach them and bring their leadership skills up to the next level.

"As your leaders attempt to solve these difficult problems, you should encourage them to have post-game reviews with their teams. In the same manner that athletic coaches would do in a post-game review, sometimes they might directly instruct their team, but other times they might get team members to say what they, themselves, could have done differently."

Joe is jotting something on his note pad. He looks up and says, "It appears I will be working just as hard as always. But rather than trying to get it all done myself, I will spend my effort delegating my tasks and becoming coach, teacher, and mentor to my leaders. This Rite of Passage calls me to *Become a Leader of Leaders.*"

"Exactly, Joe. Exactly."

Joe's Rite of Passage:

1. In his previous session with Sagen, Joe understood he must begin to *Hand It Over.*

2. Now Joe sees that in addition to handing over tasks, he must give real leadership challenges to his key players.

3. He hears that to do this he must become a coach and mentor. This will require him to accept the unique personalities of each individual and to get them to lead through their own authentic voices, even when those voices are quite different from his.

4. Some of these leaders will be beginners, so he should start by teaching basic supervisory skills.

5. Joe learns that a good way to begin coaching leaders is to give them Technical Leadership challenges in which the team has the skills to do the task but sees it as difficult.

6. Some of Joe's leaders are already well-developed professionals, so Joe should hand them Adaptive Leadership tasks.

7. Joe acknowledges that in doing all this he is moving himself through his next Rite of Passage, *Become a Leader of Leaders.*

Sagen's Mentoring Process:

1. Sagen opens the session by stepping right into an important issue. He asks Joe about his own progress on meeting the progressive emergence of needs in his people.

2. Joe wishes his supervisors had a stronger sense of pride. Sagen views this pride issue as an outcome, so he doesn't really address it. Rather, he examines the underlying process that dampens the self-esteem of Joe's subordinate leaders: Joe's tendency to over-function. He tells Joe that Joe is doing their jobs for them.

3. Sagen is quite directive as he instructs Joe to attend their meetings and observe.

4. Sagen further instructs Joe to coach them based on their own level of leadership development. Some might need basic supervisory skills. Others will be ready for Technical Leadership, and others will be ready for Adaptive Leadership tasks.

5. When Joe says, "I don't see myself in some of them," he is revealing a trap that ensnares many leaders. He should not try to create clones of himself. Sagen advises him to allow them to lead using their own authentic voices.

6. All this work will move Joe away from being the singular leader of the organization, and to *Become a Leader of Leaders*.

Case Study:

1. Joe says he would like to see more self-confidence and pride among his subordinate leaders. Sagen does not address this issue directly but rather he jumps to the notion that Joe tends to over-function as a leader. Has Sagen made a mistake in his logic here?

2. Do you tend to over-function at work, with your family, or in your personal relationships? If so, has this been adaptive? Have there been times it has been counterproductive?

3. Sagen tells Joe that to *Become a Leader of Leaders* he must actively coach his subordinate leaders, but likewise, they need to be receptive and coachable. Have you been asked to lead or supervise people who are not coachable? This could be at work or in volunteer organizations. What characteristics do coachable vs. non-coachable people have?

4. When Joe says that he does not see himself in some of them, Sagen encourages him to let his people lead with their own authentic voices. What are the types of personalities that would make you unable to mentor someone?

5. Sagen advises Joe to have his lower-level leaders try to get their group to tackle a task that requires Technical Leadership. He suggests that Joe not help them until after the fact. However, Sagen advises him to pre-coach his more advanced leaders as they embark on an Adaptive Leadership task. Please explain why Sagen suggests not to pre-coach one group and to, indeed, pre-coach another.

6. Sagen tells Joe in this Rite of Passage he must *Become a Leader of Leaders*. Hasn't Joe already accomplished this? Please defend your answer.

Chapter Twelve

Twelfth Rite of Passage: Make Them Partners

Joe begins the conversation. "Sagen, six months have passed since our last visit and much has changed. During these months a national competitor has targeted almost every single one of our most long-standing accounts. I use the word 'targeted' because it is true. Their tactics are ruthless. They follow our trucks so they know all of our accounts. Somehow, they have cloned our replacement parts and are selling them more cheaply than our own cost. They have made their own CAD drawings of our most popular conveyor designs. They have hired away several of our key salespeople and have given them impressive raises. Every time we submit a competitive bid, they undercut us in price. We are losing treasured accounts every day. This is not normal competition. We are under attack and it has been brutal."

Sagen replies, "It sounds, indeed, like you are under attack. Any idea what precipitated this?"

"I have heard their new CEO is out to make a name for himself."

"Will they be able to continue this price-cutting forever?"

Joe replies, "Absolutely not. They don't operate very efficiently and we believe their cost structure is much higher than ours."

"This is called 'buying the market'. They seek to acquire new accounts by offering tremendously low prices. However, they hope to increase those prices as time goes by," Sagen says.

"Makes sense."

Sagen asks, "Whose responsibility is it to fix this?"

"Mine, of course."

Sagen says, "That is correct. This problem might relate to the work you are doing already. Please allow me ask you how your work has been progressing regarding your *Becoming a Leader of Leaders*?"

"It has gone well so far. This has been perhaps the most difficult leadership development work that you have asked me to do. You've told me I can accomplish more by doing less. I was quite uncomfortable in the early stages of all this. At first, I didn't think it would work. However, as I moved along, I could see there was a magnifier effect going on. My subordinate leaders were eager to take on more responsibility and show what they could do. I've been quite impressed. It seemed the only one who was having trouble with this was me. I still find it hard to let go."

"Ah yes, Joe, this will be an ongoing self-development project for you. It sounds as if your team is responding nicely and you're handling it quite well so far. In your work to *Become a Leader of Leaders*, have you or your team created a plan regarding this predatory competitor?"

Joe says, "I have approached this using an Adaptive Leadership format. I have told my key people we are in a situation we have never been in before and therefore we need to make decisions that we've never been required to make. I told them we need to *Enter the Cone of Uncertainty* once again. Their response has been positive and impressive. They remember the various times I have used the terms Adaptive Leadership and *Enter the Cone of Uncertainty* in the past, and they seem ready to join me in that uncertainty."

Sagen says, "I am impressed that you have come so far in your leadership development. I am equally impressed with your team. So, where do things stand now regarding your firm's response to this competitor?"

"They have recommended two things. First, based on our Relationship Platform and the fact that we have operated with honesty and integrity for all these years, they suggested that each salesperson simply go out to every account and explain what is happening. Just tell the truth and explain that we do not believe the competition can keep its prices this low for very long. Remind them of the great service we give them and how many times we have done them a favor. Second, my senior team further suggested that we could strengthen our own Efficient Platform in light of the fact that it has been several years since we conducted projects to improve our internal efficiencies. We will not participate in irresponsible pricing or a price war, but we do believe we can lower our cost structure once again, and this will allow us some flexibility with our prices."

Sagen says, "In order for you to achieve these new efficiencies you will need partners."

"Partners?"

"Yes, partners."

Joe asks, "Do you have anyone in mind for this partnership?"

Sagen replies, "In fact, I do. I recommend you partner with everyone who works for you. This Rite of Passage is called, *Make Them Partners.*"

Joe asks, "Are you recommending an Employee Stock Ownership Plan?"

"Well, Joe, an ESOP is not what I had in mind, but perhaps you could think about that. There has been a revolution going on in business and it began in Springfield, Missouri. A fellow there named Jack Stack at Springfield Remanufacturing Corporation was in far worse financial shape than you are at this moment. It appeared there was no way for him to succeed. So, he educated every employee about company financials such as the cost of goods sold, depreciation, the cost of waste, and other operational measures."

Sagen continues, "Mr. Stack had the belief that he needed to do more than simply report the level of profit or loss because measures of profit and loss are lagging indicators. They only show the results of what everyone has already done. So he looked for costs that go on as processes occur inside the plant. He listed each employee's key performance indicators or KPIs, and only chose KPIs that connected the employee's actions to the overall performance of the company. The results were stunning. Employees operating machines began to think in the same terms that managers and leaders normally do. They began to operate extremely efficiently and their productivity increased dramatically. It is one of the greatest business turnaround stories. Stack has written a highly credible book on the topic, *The Great Game of Business*. This is an extremely popular business book and I strongly recommend you read it. You might not do everything exactly the way he did, but I believe the book will influence you." [21]

Joe asks, "All this was accomplished simply by educating the employees?"

Sagen continues to teach. "We must assume your people take pride in their skills and attitudes, and that they cherish their customer relations. However, most of them really don't know the forces in play that determine the success or failure of the company nor whether the company is performing well or poorly. This is because most companies keep these numbers top-secret. It is as if the leaders assume the employees could not understand the complexity of the numbers. Mr. Stack insists that these are not complex numbers and the employees can, indeed, understand them. [22]

"Using Mr. Stack's methods, you should be able to ask a forklift driver in your warehouse whether or not the forklift should be replaced. She might tell you that the $40,000 cost of the forklift including interest on the loan will be paid out over 10 years, and this might appear to reduce company gross profits by $4,000 per year. However, the forklift she is driving breaks down at least once every month and therefore warehouse items must be handpicked and carried to the loading dock for two days each time this happens. The cost of this low productivity is far more than $4,000 per year, and the cost of repairs to the current forklift averages $9,000 per year. After 10 years there will be no more purchasing cost. She would say the return on investment will happen in three years if we account for the cost of repairs, and the financial benefit to the company increases even more after the tenth year. This forklift driver would recommend you buy the forklift."

Joe replies, "That's amazing."

Sagen continues, "Do you remember when we last spoke, I suggested you read *The Four Disciplines of Execution*?"

"Yes. It discusses in some detail how to pick important goals, select lead measures, create a scoreboard, and generate a culture of accountability."

Sagen says, "The concepts in *The Four Disciplines of Execution* support Stack's approach. Stack says we must teach the employees the game they are in, how to keep score, and how to win the game. Everyone loves to win but most employees don't know the real things that make a company win."

"Sagen, how do we determine what winning is?"

"You set a threshold, which is not the same thing as profit. However, I have seen companies report measures such as profit per employee, and this seems to work."

Joe asks, "What motivates the employees to play this game?"

Sagen replies, "Most people like to win games just to win. Think about card games, board games, and local sports leagues. We just like to win. Beyond that, it would be wise to include an incentive. Here, I am not suggesting a Christmas bonus. Employees will only see this as a gift, and often will feel that it is just not enough anyway. I am suggesting a real incentive such as 8.3% of their base pay if the threshold is met. That may not sound like much, but it is one month's pay. Likewise, 16.7% of base pay is two months' pay. If you explain it in terms of monthly pay, they will understand and it will motivate them."

Sagen continues, "I have one more book to recommend on this topic, titled *Ownership Thinking* by Brad Hams. [23] It focuses on how to foster a sense of responsibility in every employee. Hams goes into great detail about how to build accountability throughout the organization. He spells out many examples of Key Performance Indicators (KPIs) which might help you in your planning. It points to concrete steps various companies have taken."

"This sounds like a huge undertaking," Joe says.

"Huge, indeed, but you and your organization are ready for this. You are ready for them to have ownership thinking. You are ready to *Make Them Partners* in the performance of your business."

"My next leadership Rite of Passage, *Make them Partners*."

Joe's Rite of Passage:

1. Joe encounters a problem that he cannot solve alone. Because of his history of working on his own leadership development with Sagen, he is wise enough to ask his team to *Enter the Cone of Uncertainty*.
2. Joe is now a sophisticated leader who is comfortable with himself. He is at a point of maturity where he can comfortably partner with his employees. He can show them expenses and profits. This would have been impossible for Joe at an earlier stage of his leadership development.
3. Joe listens carefully as Sagen describes open book management. He sees how some form of this can benefit his organization.
4. Joe sees that this Rite of Passage, *Make Them Partners*, will be a huge undertaking. However, he has become accustomed to these long-term developmental projects.

Sagen's Mentoring Process:

1. Sagen is impressed with how far Joe has come in developing his leadership abilities.

2. He observes that Joe is comfortable asking his team to engage in Adaptive Leadership.

3. Sagen is pleased that Joe's team builds its response to a predatory competitor using the Relationship Platform and Efficient Platform strategies which have carried the firm so well for all these years.

4. It might appear that Sagen is simply teaching Joe how open book management works. However, at a deeper level he is really teaching Joe how to extend his personal influence by getting higher-level work done through others. He is moving Joe along on this overall mission, *Become a Leader of Leaders*.

5. Sagen sees that Joe and his organization are ready for this work because Joe has tried diligently to *Become a Leader of Leaders*.

6. Within the mission of Become a *Leader of Leaders*, this Rite of Passage is called *Make Them Partners*.

Case Study:

1. Joe is experiencing the shock of an unexpected attack on his company. He has endured recessions and other economic impacts, but this one seems to be the result of foul play by a competitor. Is it foul play?

2. In response to this threat, the leadership team has recommended Joe strengthen the firm's Relationship Platform and its Efficient Platform. Do you believe they are blindly just continuing to do what has worked in the past?

3. This Rite of Passage is called, *Make Them Partners*. Sagen suggests that Joe use some form of open book management in which the activities of each department are measured according to the financial contribution of those activities. Many managers are afraid to open the books, even slightly. Why is this?

4. Would it be possible to *Make Them Partners* without keeping score, sharing financials, and offering bonuses? How would that work?

5. Once again Joe has presented one problem but Sagen's solution appears, at first glance, to be unrelated to the problem. How would keeping score and sharing financial information help KC Miller Conveyor ward off this predatory competitor?

6. Could it be possible to competently *Become a Leader of Leaders* without making your subordinate leaders partners? Could this extend to an entire organization becoming partners? Please discuss your position.

7. Most workplaces have some type of hierarchical authority. What difficulties might Joe encounter as he moves through this Rite of Passage, *Make Them Partners*?

Chapter Thirteen

Thirteenth Rite of Passage: Empower Your Leaders to Build Their Teams

Ever the student, Joe sits before his mentor and waits to see what guidance Sagen will render this time. They sip their tea and for a moment all is quiet. Joe observes again how noticeably advanced Sagen's aging process has become. Still, Sagen's mind is sharp, and he is able to expose the subtle nuances of every circumstance. Joe takes this moment to remind himself how grateful he is to have received the gift of Sagen's wisdom through the years.

"Joe, when we last spoke, I presented you with yet another leadership Rite of Passage, *Make Them Partners*. This is part of your third mission, *Become a Leader of Leaders*. Can you tell me anything about how this has been going?"

"Yes, of course," says Joe. "It has been only three months since we last spoke, and we are quite aware that creating an atmosphere of real partnership will be a long process. I have had my senior leaders read *The Great Game of Business*, *The Four Disciplines of Execution*, and *Ownership Thinking*. We have been having weekly video conferences to talk about the content of those books and to figure out how to operationalize those concepts. All this has gone well despite the fact that a few of my people have made comments about being back in school again."

Sagen interrupts, "I am impressed. You have created a learning organization."

"It became a learning organization long ago, Sagen, thanks to you. Regarding my effort to *Make Them Partners*, what surprises me is the wide range of success or lack of success the various locations have had, even at this early stage. It doesn't make sense that some should do so well and others so poorly, given the fact that they are all executing the same basic steps. There seems to be good enthusiasm for this program at all locations. The employees and middle managers are picking the right goals, keeping score, and examining how their own operations contribute to those scores. We have established a bonus system in which the various teams can be given cash that is measured in terms of workdays. I would think this should produce similar results across the board, but the results have been extremely variable. Quite honestly, some locations are establishing a noticeable attitude of partnership but others simply are not."

"Are you satisfied that your senior leaders at each location are competent?"

"Yes."

"Well, perhaps it is time to address another Rite of Passage."

"So soon?"

"These passages call to you when they are ready, not when you are ready. Right?"

"Indeed, they do."

Sagen continues, "If you have capable leaders and similar processes, there should be some small amount of variability between locations, but you say you have great variability. This means it is time to look beyond just the question of how well your leaders are leading and ask whether the various work groups within their organizations have become good teams. Focus less on the leader and more on team functioning. Remember, this third mission calls you to *Become a*

Leader of Leaders. The next Rite of Passage within that mission is *Help Them Build Their Teams.*"

"Okay Sagen, but I don't see how we can have a good leader and at that same location not have a good team. Don't good leaders always create good teams?"

Sagen answers, "Let me ask a question to shed some light on this subject. In American football, haven't there been several amazing quarterbacks who were gifted and impressive, but their teams were just terrible?"

"Yes, I can think of a few."

"Well, this is similar. Being a great leader does not guarantee a high-functioning team. To have a great team, the leader will need to address those variables that distinguish high-functioning teams from teams that are lower-functioning. Too many leaders try to generate a lot of enthusiasm and energy in the hope that this will create a great team. It rarely works. As they say, 'you have to pull the right levers.' What creates success here is carefully influencing the variables that build high-functioning teams."

Joe has his pad of paper out, ready to take notes. "So, what are those variables?"

"Right Joe, what are those variables? Can you tell me about a high-functioning team within your organization?"

"Yes. Jane Davis, the vice president of sales, has done a remarkable job of turning around the culture and competency of her team. If you recall, not long after you and I started working together, and I had encouraged my senior team to *Enter the Cone of Uncertainty* in order to find a new strategy, she was the one who said we should ask what Dillinger would do. She was new to us then and had inherited a very dysfunctional sales team."

Sagen says, "I do recall, but what is it about how her team functions now that makes it a better team than it was back then? As you answer this, you will be describing the traits of high-functioning teams."

"As I recall," Joe says, "years ago she commented that every time she tried to point out how something could be done more efficiently, the sales employee would take it personally, as if he or she had been insulted. Now it is just the opposite. A critique about how something could be improved creates an engaged discussion, and everybody joins in. The results of her turnaround have been remarkable."

Sagen asks, "What does this tell you?"

"A lot, I think. It tells me they allow open and honest debate so things can improve, just the way a great athletic team would."

"What is needed in order for the team to have this open and honest debate?"

Joe contemplates the question for a moment. "I suppose this requires trust. They need to feel comfortable that they can admit mistakes and it will not sink their careers."

"Joe, it sounds as if you have been reading Patrick Lencioni's *The Advantage.* [13] This is all in that book."

"I read it long ago, as you will recall."

"What other characteristics does the high-functioning sales team have now that it didn't before?"

"After they debate a topic, they all get behind the new initiative and pretend they were unanimously in favor of it, even if they weren't, behind closed doors," Joe says.

Sagen says, "Yes, the common phrase for this is 'disagree and commit.' This phrase was coined by Sun Microsystems founder Scott McNealy. First, the leader encourages some disagreement, some debate. This allows the team to fully examine the issue. Once the debate is over, even if the vote had not been unanimous, the entire leadership team puts on a united front."

Joe replies, "That's how it is now in her department, but it was just the opposite a long time ago."

"It sounds like Jane has been working to develop her department into a high-functioning team. Can you think of anything else high-functioning teams do?"

Joe thinks for a moment and says, "Yes. I don't know if Jane's team does this, but high-functioning sports teams and military units do a post-game analysis. I must admit we have not done enough of that with our headquarters teams."

"Indeed, they do, Joe. They take the time to look over the game tapes. Do you remember when you and I talked about this, including making use of root cause analysis methods like the Fishbone Diagram?"

"Yes, I recall. I think this is an incredible team builder, but I am afraid some of the steps we are talking about here are too basic, too simple."

Sagen replies, "They are quite basic and easy for us to talk about, but they are difficult to execute. They will be a challenge for your leaders."

"Okay," Joe says, "but are there some high-functioning team development steps that are more advanced?"

"Certainly, there are. If you have a team that appears to be functioning well already, you might question whether each team member takes full responsibility for the forward-falling dominoes with every decision he or she makes. Teams that are filled with members who do this are impressively high-functioning."

Joe asks, "The forward-falling dominoes?"

"Yes," Sagen says. "Suppose a customer calls and asks for an additional product that he or she had not ordered, and it is needed today. Your firm accommodates this type of thing as a way of building deeper relationships. When a production supervisor simply stops manufacturing the parts for a different customer's order so he or she can please this customer, does he or she look to see what the ripple effect of this decision will be? Will his or her actions take products out of production that were intended for other customers? Will it impact the warehouse? Will the last truck of the day leave without some other customer's order on it? Every person in every workplace makes these decisions every day, but usually they do not look to see what the subsequent impacts of these decisions will be. In high-functioning teams, all teammates study this carefully as they move along. Frontline team members take responsibility for the forward-falling dominoes and they don't simply assume this is the responsibility of the boss."

Joe continues to write on his notepad. He says, "We have discussed seven characteristics of high-functioning teams. Here they are, as I understand it:

1. Trust
2. Ability to feel comfortable and admit mistakes
3. Open and honest debate
4. Disagree and commit
5. Post-game analysis
6. Root cause analysis
7. Taking responsibility for the forward falling dominoes"

Joe says, "Sagen, I am a little concerned. You and I have listed these qualities of high-functioning teams, but I believe there are many more. In fact, there may be many that I won't be able to point out."

Sagen replies, "Don't worry about this. Let the student be your teacher. In fact, tell your leaders to let the students be their teachers. As they observe the team, the team itself will show the leader what work it needs to do. Neither you nor they should go in with a pre-scripted agenda and try to impose it on all teams. Each team will have its own work to do, and the team will reveal this work to the leader."

Joe replies, "Just as I have revealed to you the work I have needed to do, all these years?"

"Exactly."

Sagen continues, "You have done well on your journey toward becoming an extraordinary leader. The focus now becomes the team and how well it functions. This Rite of Passage is *Empower Your Leaders to Build Their Teams.*"

Joe's Rite of Passage:

1. Joe's attachment to Sagen is obvious as he thinks about how grateful he is to have received Sagen's wisdom over the years.
2. Ever the engineer, Joe can't understand how the different locations can have such wide-ranging results if they are all implementing the same programs. He believes the same input variables should create the same output in every location.
3. He asks how it is possible to have a good leader who does not produce a good team.
4. Joe is ready for Sagen when Joe asks him what the traits of a high-functioning team are. Sagen hands that question right back to Joe.
5. As he describes Jane Davis' turnaround of the warehouse team, it becomes clear that Joe is teaching himself. He is organizing his observations of the warehouse team in a way that allows the traits of a high-functioning team to emerge.
6. Joe gets it: This Rite of Passage calls him to focus less on the leader and more on the team. It is called, *Empower Your Leaders to Build Their Teams.*

Sagen's Mentoring Process:

1. Sagen has created a healthy mentor-mentee relationship here. He knows Joe is grateful for the guidance he has received from him over these many years.

2. Most likely, Sagen has much gratitude for this relationship as well. It is immensely rewarding for a mentor to see his student put the mentor's advice to use as he travels the various missions and Rites of Passage toward becoming an extraordinary leader. They both share the joy of Joe's success.

3. Sagen says something that doesn't make sense at first glance. He tells Joe that being a great leader doesn't guarantee a high-functioning team.

4. Sagen is implying that one can separate the level of leader functioning from the level of team functioning (but Sagen does know the two are intertwined). He suggests Joe look at these two factors separately simply so Joe can more clearly focus on the level of team functioning.

5. When Joe asks what the variables are that create high-functioning teams Sagen uses an old and familiar mentoring tool. He returns the question to Joe.

6. Sagen gets Joe to list the traits of high-functioning teams.

7. Sagen knows this is not an exhaustive list. When Joe asks for a more complete list, Sagen says to let the student be the teacher. He assures Joe that as each team moves along it will reveal the work it needs to do.

8. He tells Joe, *Empower Your Leaders to Build Their Teams.*

Case Study:

1. Are you acting as a mentor? What is the level of attachment between you and your mentee? Has your mentee had some success? Do you gain some joy when you observe his or her success?
2. Have you ever felt you were a good leader but you were in charge of a team that was not high-functioning? What was that like? What were your sources of frustration?
3. Have you ever worked to turn an ordinary organization into a high-functioning team? What steps did you take? What frustrations did you encounter?
4. Sagen teases some information out of Joe about the traits of high-functioning teams. Please comment on how your team can display any of the following traits:
   1. Trust
   2. Ability to feel comfortable and admit mistakes
   3. Open and honest debate
   4. Disagree and commit
   5. Post-game analysis
   6. Root cause analysis
   7. Taking responsibility for the forward falling dominoes
5. Is the above list complete? What are some other traits of high-functioning teams?
6. Would you agree that building these competencies into a team is easy for the mentor to say, but difficult for the mentee to accomplish?

Fourth Mission: Master the Psychology of Leadership

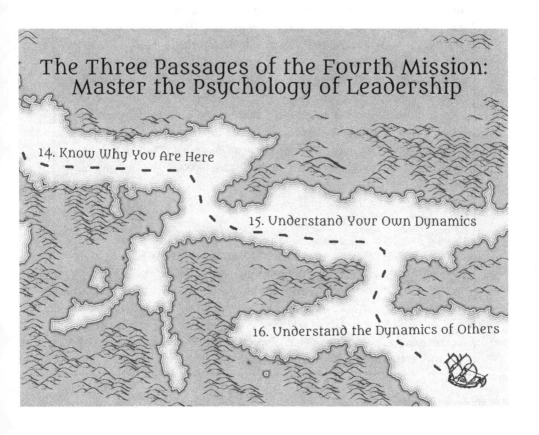

The Three Passages of the Fourth Mission:
Master the Psychology of Leadership

14. Know Why You Are Here

15. Understand Your Own Dynamics

16. Understand the Dynamics of Others

Special Note to the Reader:

During this mission, Sagen probes into Joe's personality and individual psychology. These conversations occurred early in the course of Sagen's work with Joe. We begin by jumping back to a time when Joe was 25 years old.

Of course, helping a mentee look inward is an ongoing part of mentoring. These conversations are presented here as a separate section of the book in order to make a more cohesive argument about the importance of psychology and leadership. However, in real-life mentoring, these topics are usually sprinkled throughout the entire course of the consultations.

In the pages that follow, you will see that Sagen is skilled at knowing where to look to uncover Joe's personality dynamics and emotional habits. You will also see, because this is leadership coaching and not psychotherapy, that Sagen does not attempt to do a deep dive into those psychological processes. He simply wants Joe to become more aware of how he works and how his own emotional needs and habits influence his leadership skills. Nothing more.

As a leader I hope this examination of Joe's psychology prompts you to look at some of your own dynamics.

As a leadership coach or someone who supervises other managers, you may wonder how deep to dive. A good rule of thumb is simply to ask open-ended questions and the person will supply the insights. Unless you are a psychologist or other mental health professional it is unwise to go too deep beneath the surface on all of this. Having said that, I think your client or supervisee will benefit greatly from a shallow but supportive examination of how his or her behavior patterns influence his or her leadership challenges.

Chapter Fourteen

Fourteenth Rite of Passage: Know Why You Are Here

Sagen begins the conversation, "I was quite impressed with your insightfulness when I asked you to tell me about yourself. You talked about being an only child, taking flying lessons in high school, and being a medevac pilot. These are all important parts of who you are. Can you tell me more about any of that?"

Joe sits quietly for a moment, frowns, and says, "Honestly, I don't know what else to say."

Sagen says, "I think it might be more comfortable for you if I were to just ask you some questions which are a little more focused. Would that be all right?"

Joe has regained his posture. "Yes, of course."

Sagen says, "I am impressed with your achievements, and I can see you are a good man, but the question I have been wanting to ask you is, why are you here?"

"As I had told you, I am here because your grandson David told me you help businesses and I need some help."

"Joe, when I asked why you are here, I didn't mean to ask why you are sitting in front of me. I meant, why are you where you are in your life? Why are you a 25-year-old ex-medevac pilot, cross country runner, company president?"

"Oh, why am I where I am in my life?"

"Yes."

Joe says, "Well, I guess I always thought I would graduate from college and join my father's company."

"Okay, I see, but you certainly have the credentials to have pursued a different career, right?"

Joe replies, "So you are asking why I came back to the family business, what my motive was?"

"That's a good way to put it."

Joe says, "Well, I think only children are kind of like little adults. You know, they are spoken to like they are adults even when they are very young and the conversation at the dinner table always includes them. But even though this was the case with me, I always knew I was not as capable as my parents. I was a kid, after all, so I felt somehow inadequate. I always tried my best, especially for my father. Perhaps I thought if I could join the family business and do a great job, he would begin to see me as capable and competent, like him."

Sagen says, "This makes sense. But it sounds as if it is not working out that way for you, really."

Joe sounds frustrated, "Not working out that way? As soon as I joined him, my father died! Now I am steering this company right off a cliff."

Sagen asks, "Is the company really going over a cliff?"

"No, but it does not look good."

Sagen asks, "And this is not what you had bargained for."

"No."

"Okay, please let me pursue two lines of questioning with you. My first line of questioning is based on the idea that in our lives we should always strive to understand why we are where we are. So, in your case, you have told me you joined KC Miller Conveyor to obtain the approval and respect of your father. However, he died and so you will never get the thing you were striving to obtain. Is my logic sound here?"

"Yes, that makes sense."

"Very good, but now that you are here, running this company, and in light of the fact that your father can't give you his approval, I must ask, is there any other legitimate reason for you to remain the president of this company?"

This question surprises Joe and he hesitates before speaking.

Joe responds, "Yes, I think so. In our previous interview you called me a helper. I think this is true. I do like to take care of people who are injured or at risk. That was what being a medevac helicopter pilot was about. Perhaps I don't want to see my teammates and employees lose their jobs. I don't want to see their families lose their homes. I feel the weight of this responsibility. More than that, because I am so inexperienced, I sometimes wonder if I have the wisdom to know how to lead this injured enterprise."

Sagen continues, "I understand. I do have a second line of questioning. I believe that when you were telling me about your background you said you didn't like contact sports. Is that right?"

"Yes."

Sagen asks, "So, please tell me. Is business a contact sport?"

Joe says nothing.

"Joe?"

Joe replies, "Yes. It is a contact sport for sure. It is intense, and I will say it can be lethal. People's lives can be ruined. It can be quite vicious."

Sagen asks, "So, can you work through some logic as to why you are where you are now?"

Joe replies. "The reason I am here now is not the same reason I initially came back to my father's firm. The reason I have stayed and will continue to stay is to help and protect my employees. I can say this is a worthy mission for me." Joe adds, "Who knows, maybe this will be the one contact sport I will come to enjoy."

Sagen says, "Joe, you have embarked on a new mission called *Master the Psychology of Leadership*. Of course, your leadership ability has much to do with your own psychology. To gain deeper understanding of your psychology, you must begin with this Rite of Passage. I call it, *Know Why You Are Here*."

Joe is quiet for a moment.

Sagen asks, "Would it be all right if we look again at who Joe Miller is, from time to time?"

"Yes. I think that might be helpful."

Joe's Rite of Passage:

1. Twenty-five-year-old Joe has many doubts about whether he is the right man for the job of leading his company through this crisis. However, he has not verbalized these doubts quite this frankly to anyone until this day.
2. At an unconscious level, Joe gradually becomes aware that this doubt will surface as this conversation with Sagen progress. This explains why this is a difficult session for him.
3. Joe commits to his own personal mission. He will remain the leader to ensure the wellbeing of his teammates and employees.

Sagen's Mentoring Process:

1. While entering this topic, Sagen is friendly but not overly so. He puts Joe to work quickly. He asks Joe why he is where he is in his life.
2. Knowing Joe is an engineer, Sagen uses a logic model to work with him. This logic brings Joe to commit to his mission of taking care of his people.
3. Sagen is elderly, and therefore he wonders if Joe will view him as a father figure. If so, he will expect Joe to start the relationship with an attempt to please him.

Case Study:

1. Joe finds himself in a painful situation. What is it about his psychological makeup that causes this to be more painful for him than it might be for someone else?

2. When Joe announces that he is steering his company "right off a cliff," Sagen has two obvious directions this conversation can go:
    a. He could ask Joe whether he has a tendency to blame himself for things that are out of his control.
    b. He could just get Joe to do a reality check by asking him if the company is really going off a cliff.

   Sagen choses to do a reality check. Why? Why does Sagen avoid examining the self-blame issue here?

3. Sagen walks Joe back to the question of why he is still leading this company despite the fact that his father is gone. Joe says the value he brings is to help his employees and save jobs. He says, "maybe this will be the one contact sport I will come to enjoy." What is Sagen trying to accomplish in this interchange?

Chapter Fifteen

Fifteenth Rite of Passage: Understand Your Own Dynamics

Joe starts the session, "Sagen, I was a little nervous about coming here last time, but you were very kind and helped me sort through the difficult issue of what my contribution will be at KC Miller Conveyor. Coming here today was a lot easier."

Sagen thanks Joe for the compliment and asks how his business is doing.

Joe replies, "Nothing has improved. I am working on *Entering the Cone of Uncertainty.*"

"How is that going?"

Joe continues, "I can see I should not just go through the uncertainty of my circumstance all by myself. I should draw my other leaders into it."

"How do you feel about that?"

Joe replies, "I don't think it will work. I think they all like placing this responsibility on me."

Sagen says, "I see, and although I'm sure they would like you to shoulder this burden, I asked how you feel about that and you told me what you think. Can you say something about how you feel?"

Joe is quiet for a moment while he processes this request. He says, "I would say that at a feeling level, uncertainty makes me anxious. When I don't know what to do, I start to feel nervous and can even get a sick stomach."

"Do you feel this way much of the time these days?"

"Yes, all the time."

"So would having a plan help? Sometimes just having a plan removes some of the uncertainty."

Joe says, "I am sure it would, but I don't know how to fix the American economy when it is in a recession."

Sagen asks, "Do you remember that I suggested a plan?"

Joe answers, "Yes, you have told me to prompt my team to *Enter the Cone of Uncertainty* and the plan will emerge."

Sagen says, "Joe, I have already told you what the plan is. The plan is to use the *Cone of Uncertainty* as a tool to draw your team together and to collectively come up with a strategy that will work."

Joe asks, "So *Entering the Cone of Uncertainty* is the plan?"

"Sounds like it to me."

Sagen continues, "Can we say that if I am to understand your psychology, I should know that you do not like uncertainty?"

"Yes."

"How far does this go?"

"Well, it doesn't go too far. I don't worry about the weather, gasoline prices, or getting stuck in a traffic jam, if that's what you mean."

"So, when does this uncertainty bother you?"

"Only when the consequences of that uncertainty can be a big deal. But let me ask you, Sagen, what leadership advice would you give a guy like me on this issue?"

Sagen considers this a fair request, so he answers, "I would say you can reduce your anxiety over the course of your career if you make plans. These could be strategic plans, operational plans, or project plans, but just having a plan will make you more comfortable."

Sagen continues, "I must tell you there is something that puzzles me. You were a medevac pilot in a very dangerous environment. Of course, you would have flight plans. But those plans often changed. Wasn't this an environment filled with uncertainty?"

Joe attempts to minimize, "Well it all sounds more dangerous than it was."

Sagen doesn't allow this. He says, "Joe, it was extremely dangerous."

Joe sits quietly for what seems to be a long time. He says, "Yes, it was extremely dangerous. Sagen, as I have told you, in that environment I was able to turn off my feelings completely."

"Completely?"

"Yes. When the bullets started flying or when small rounds would hit my chopper, I felt like what I was going through was not real, as if I were an actor in a movie or a play; like I was not really me. It was a strange sensation."

Sagen asks, "And when you got back to base, would this complete absence of emotion continue?"

"No, I would return to normal very quickly."

Sagen says, "Well, what we are working on here is getting you to know your own psychological dynamics so maybe we should talk about this for a moment. Would that be okay?"

Joe replies, "Maybe I need to. You have called this going third person."

Sagen speaks cautiously here. "Joe, after our first conversation I began researching this and I found a case study that had been reported in a professional journal. It was about a fellow who was a first responder and was, himself, in many dangerous and gruesome circumstances. He described his lack of emotions exactly the same way you describe yours in combat. You see, going third person is just a way of dealing with conflict or uncertainty in an objective way in the ordinary course of business. Seasoned leaders do this naturally. According to that journal, what you experienced in combat is called a dissociative response. It is much more powerful than going third person."

"Is it a bad thing?"

"Not necessarily. But according to the research, what seems unusual here is that we typically find dissociative responses in people who operate at a primitive level in other areas of their lives, and you don't seem to do that."

Joe asks, "Wait. Do all people who have these dissociative responses operate at a primitive level?"

Sagen says, "The research says no, not all."

Joe says, "Maybe it was just my mind's way of allowing me to fly the chopper, get my wounded out, and for us all to survive."

"Not maybe, Joe. Definitely. And it was highly adaptive. Further, it tells us you will be able to deal with your current situation well. You have good reflexive instincts."

Joe seems to be thinking this over.

Sagen says, "We must consider the fact that leadership is certainly one of the most complex of human endeavors. It does help if you know yourself as you go through your leadership career. What else can you tell me about your psychology?"

Joe responds, "I'm not sure what you are looking for. I see myself as a nice guy. I try to be liked by everyone. Overall, I would see this as a leadership strength, wouldn't you?

Sagen does not answer this question. He asks, "Does this desire to be liked ever get in your way?"

Joe answers, "Maybe, like when I should be having a difficult conversation with someone who is performing poorly. I tend to procrastinate on that and I'm not sure I do it very well. Maybe deep down, I'm afraid the person won't like me."

Sagen asks, "May I ask about a different topic? Do you think growing up as an only child influenced you?"

Joe responds, "Yes. Beyond what I've already told you, I think I need to belong to a group. That's what being in the brass section was in high school and that's something I got out of the army, great fellowship."

Sagen says, "We are working on your new mission, *Master the Psychology of Leadership*. Within this mission it seems we have found your next Rite of Passage. Simply, we call it *Understand Your Own Dynamics*. It is intended to make you more aware of your own needs and how you approach your team. So, may I ask, how do you think this need for fellowship might influence your leadership?

Joe replies, "I don't know, exactly. Maybe I will come to see my employees and coworkers all as family and find a great deal of closeness there. At least I hope so."

"I hope so, too, Joe."

Joe's Rite of Passage:

1. Joe talks about how uncertainty gives him great discomfort. He makes sure Sagen knows that this is limited to times of high risk.
2. He accepts the idea that simply making a plan might calm him. We will see him become a plan maker as part of his leadership development.
3. Joe is curious about the concept of a dissociative response. He worries that Sagen might see him as primitive. He is relieved to hear that it appears to be adaptive in his case.
4. He reveals that his greatest need in his work environment is fellowship and he wants his colleagues to become "family."
5. He is fully engaged when Sagen says this mission is to *Understand Your Own Dynamics*.

Sagen's Mentoring Process:

1. Sagen notices that Joe begins the session by giving him a gift as he says, "You were very kind and helped me sort through the difficult issue of what my contribution will be at KC Miller Conveyor. Coming here today was a lot easier."

2. Sagen ignores the fact that this compliment is a gift.

3. Sagen sees that Joe limits his discussion of uncertainty to the topic of attempting to get his coworkers to *Enter the Cone of Uncertainty*. Joe does not say anything about any other possible source of uncertainty, like Joe's lack of experience. Sagen allows this and doesn't push into other sources of uncertainty.

4. Sagen doesn't permit Joe to minimize the dangers he faced as a medivac helicopter pilot. Here, he becomes quite direct with Joe.

5. As Joe describes his dissociative response, Sagen tells him quite frankly that it was adaptive.

6. Sagen jumps from one psychological topic to another. He does not wish to look into Joe's deeper psychology. He simply wants Joe to identify some of the internal processes that may influence his leadership skills, such as a need for fellowship and his need to care for others. This is leadership coaching, not psychotherapy.

7. When Joe says he wants his colleagues to become family, this occurs at a time in this story prior to when his friend, Controller Kathleen Anderson, betrays him. Note that Sagen does not lecture Joe to beware of possible internal saboteurs.

8. Regarding colleagues becoming family, Sagen simply says, "I hope so, too, Joe."

Case Study:

1. Of course, the first source of Joe's uncertainty is the need to find an adaptive strategic response to his company's struggles. Could a second source be that he still feels uncertain about whether he is competent to lead this company? What should he do about either source of uncertainty? Would you have encouraged him to discuss his doubts about his leadership skills?

2. Should Sagen have interpreted to Joe that his compliment was a gift? Should he have asked him what he was trying to gain by offering this gift? He chose not to do so. Why?

3. About planning, what is the relationship between leadership and planning? Can a leader move forward without a plan? What is an adhocracy? What is a bureaucracy? Many professions, such as accounting, design, surgery, and architecture require great precision. Mechanical engineering does, also. Would it be accurate for us to assume a person with Joe's engineering background and need to avoid uncertainty would tend to over-plan?

4. What if this were a story about a person with a different personality type? What are some possible needs that could tend to enhance and/ or disrupt his or her leadership? What types of personalities tend to underemphasize planning?

5. Joe speaks with some innocence when he says he wants his colleagues to be family. Should Sagen have warned him about the danger of betrayal that most certainly lies ahead?

Chapter Sixteen

Sixteenth Rite of Passage: Understand the Dynamics of Others

Joe begins his visit with Sagen with one simple statement. "This is not a very good time for me."

Sagen responds, "Please tell me more, Joe."

Joe replies, "In our last meeting I told you about the entire episode with Kathleen Anderson, my controller. I'm just not over it. As I told you, I really thought we were friends, and I trusted her completely. When I discovered that she cleverly ridiculed me behind my back and had been embezzling money, I took this as a personal betrayal. I still do."

Sagen says, "I can see this is very difficult for you."

Joe asks, "How could I have been so stupid? This makes me think I don't know anything about people."

Sagen replies, "I can see how you might feel that way, but it sounds like anyone could have been deceived by Kathleen. I know of many great leaders who've been fooled by this. How are you trying to change your thinking on this?"

Joe replies, "Now I can see that what you have said is true. Excessive flattery can be just as lethal as excessive criticism."

"Joe, the cost of wisdom is high."

Joe replies, "Really."

Sagen says, "Really. As I have said to you, Kathleen has moved your wisdom up to a much higher level. Now you know so much more. She took you by surprise with her excessive flattery but this will not happen to you again." Sagen continues, "Are you resentful?"

"Yes. And I recall you had said I should forgive and return to generating prosperity."

Sagen replies, "Good work to do."

Sagen offers some instruction, "Leadership is as much about knowing the psychology of the other person as it is about understanding your own psychology. When dealing with others you should begin by asking four questions about the other person:

1. What does this person need?
2. What is his or her personality?
3. Why might this person be the way he or she is?
4. Knowing all this, you should ask whether his or her personality is nourishing or toxic."

Joe says, "I believe I'll need a little explanation. Please?"

Sagen says, "Regarding the first question, 'What does this person need?' I mean, what does he or she want from the leader or the group? It might be significance, recognition, or simply to know that his or her contribution matters. There could be many other motives. Of course, you can't know everything about his or her needs, but it would help you to try to keep this in mind as you work together."

Joe replies, "Actually, I believe I can give the basic needs to anyone who is trying to do a good job."

Sagen confirms, "I believe you can."

Sagen continues, "Regarding the second question, 'What is his or her personality?' I am really asking how you would categorize this person. Let's start with some easy ones. Ask yourself whether this person is:

1. An introvert or an extrovert.
2. Orderly and methodical versus disorganized and ad hoc.
3. One who seeks deep attachments versus one who remains aloof and detached.
4. Emotionally resistant to feedback and criticism versus receptive and appreciative for the guidance."

Joe says, "It would seem strange to try to put people into categories."

Sagen replies, "All personality types come in degrees, not separate categories. We can't put most people completely in the introvert box or the extrovert box. A person isn't all introvert or all extrovert. These characteristics move along a continuum. A person might be mildly introverted or only introverted under certain circumstances."

Joe asks, "Is one better than the other? Is extroversion better than introversion?"

"Of course, there are circumstances where one is better," Sagen says. "I suppose you would like your salespeople to be extroverts, wouldn't you? And I'll bet you would like your surgeon to be orderly and methodical, right? However, I have known great salespeople who are introverted in general but remarkably extroverted when they are in the sales role. Make sense?"

Joe asks, "What about the issue regarding why a person might be the way he or she is? How can I know what causes people to be the way they are?"

Sagen says, "Mostly, you won't know. This one is quite difficult to detect. You can only guess. But don't guess too much. Having some sense of why a person is the way he or she is can give you more empathy for them. You should know that there are enduring traits that the person internalized into his or her personality long before he or she met you. These traits will remain ongoing into the future."

"So, I can't turn an introvert into an extrovert?"

"No, but you can understand that he or she is an introvert and then do your best to make him or her comfortable, so he or she can contribute. Work within his or her personality dynamics as best you can."

Joe says, "I do have a guy who over-reacts to any feedback or critique. He gets offended every time I try to offer him even the smallest guidance. What do I do about that?"

"First, just know it. Then, work within his framework. Give him a lot of praise before offering any criticism. If you want to criticize, just start by asking him how he sees a thing going and whether it is where he wants it to be. Ask how he would like to see it change. Ask what has prevented it from moving in the right direction so far. Act as if you and he are both examining the same object together. You are a mechanical engineer, so explore the subject like you both are two mechanical engineers looking at the same machinery at the same time."

Sagen continues, "If you know he overreacts, you know a lot about him already. So, why would he or anyone be overly sensitive to criticism? What hunches does this give to you?"

Joe answers, "I suppose I would look for overly critical parents or harsh coaches in his background. Something like that."

Sagen says, "Almost always this is the case."

"I see."

Sagen presents Joe with a difficult question. "As this man's leader, can you change the way he reacts to criticism? I will tell you that under this circumstance, many leaders do try to change the way the follower reacts to criticism. So, will you try to change his personality?"

Joe smiles. "No. But what do I do with this?"

Sagen answers, "Just know it. Let this knowledge guide your interactions with him. Let this knowledge modify your behavior, and then he just might let his guard down. This is where the art of psychology intersects with leadership."

Joe asks, "What did you mean by your fourth question, whether a personality is nourishing or toxic? Can the same personality be either nourishing or toxic?"

Sagen explains, "Imagine one extrovert who is always telling jokes, but these jokes are somehow at someone's expense. You sense a built-in hostility to his humor and the way he engages others. Maybe his humor always leans slightly toward bigotry or somehow toward establishing his own superiority. Sometimes he can be funny, but wouldn't you sense that overall, this is toxic to those around him?"

"Yes."

Sagen says, "So there we have a toxic extrovert. Now imagine there is another person who is very extroverted, but without this hostility. She is just a friendly individual who loves to connect with others. She is helpful and pays compliments to those around her. Like the man we were just discussing, she is an extrovert, but unlike him her extroversion nourishes your team."

Joe observes, "Not toxic."

Sagen asks, "What if you notice that through her extroversion, the second extrovert always seems to be working hard to make herself the center of the group?"

Joe asks, "Would that make her toxic?"

Sagen replies, "Not necessarily. In fact, I just might want to invite her to my Christmas party."

Joe chuckles.

Sagen continues, "This has much to do with followership. You see, Joe, this all becomes important when trying to gather followers. You need to understand not just their economic or occupational needs, but also their psychological needs. You should work to meet each person where he or she is."

Joe says, "Sagen, I was quite hesitant about discussing psychology with you, but these conversations with you have been very helpful."

Sagen replies, "I am enjoying getting to know you as well, Joe. And I can say you have made a good start on your journey toward becoming an extraordinary leader."

Joe asks, "Is this a Rite of Passage?"

"Of course it is, a very important one. It is *Understand the Dynamics of Others.*"

Joe replies, "I think I will need to work on this one for a long time."

Joe's Rite of Passage:

1. The fact that Joe begins the session by talking about Kathleen Anderson's betrayal is an indication of how deeply injured he is by this.
2. Sagen offers empathy but then segues to the topic of understanding the psychology of others. Joe allows the subject to be changed.
3. Joe listens well to the four questions.
4. He is able to see the subtleties of this topic, and he asks good questions.
5. Joe is receptive to the idea that personality dynamics come in degrees and that the same personality category can be nourishing or toxic.
6. Joe says, "I will need to work on this one for a long time."
7. Once again, Joe offers a relationship statement to Sagen when he says, "These conversations with you have been very helpful."

Sagen's Process:

1. Sagen is not surprised when Joe begins the interview by revisiting the painful story of Kathleen Anderson. He knows this kind of injury does not offer a quick recovery.
2. After giving Joe some empathic understanding, he moves on to new work.
3. Sagen offers Joe an over-simplified way of understanding how other people's psychology can work. He knows this is over-simplified but it is not his intent here to turn Joe into a psychologist. Rather, he just wants Joe to begin seeking some deeper understanding of others' personality dynamics.
4. He offers Joe four questions regarding need, personality, motive, and toxicity.
5. When Joe pays Sagen a compliment, Sagen says, "I am enjoying getting to know you as well, Joe."
6. Sagen offers Joe a new Rite of Passage, *Understanding the Dynamics of Others*. He knows this is a very long-term endeavor.

Case Study:

1. Joe is still in pain over Kathleen Anderson. Is this normal? Why can't he just move past this?

2. At a very superficial level, it would appear that Joe's injury here is simply Kathleen's betrayal. Is it possible that at a deeper level the real injury comes from Joe's new awareness that he is gullible and very easily taken advantage of? If so, does this cause him to view himself as a weak leader?

3. What do you think was really going on inside Joe regarding Kathleen? Was she simply a trusted colleague and friend? Did he have a secret crush on her? Was she a mother figure, taking care of him? Why is this injury so severe for him?

4. Do you believe he can begin his recovery from this injury by returning the firm to prosperity?

5. Do you agree that the four questions about personality dynamics are the right place to start for Joe?

6. How deeply should a leader be involved in *Understanding the Dynamics of Others*? Why should the leader care about this at all? In the end, isn't the leader's responsibility simply to accomplish goals, so perhaps he or she could just circumvent some of this?

7. Sagen tells Joe this is part of creating followership. How so?

8. Please provide some examples of people you have known (without revealing their identities or any confidential information) and how they would rate on the four questions. You may use famous people or roles actors have played.

9. For the first time, when Joe makes a relationship statement, Sagen responds by saying, "I am enjoying getting to know you as well, Joe." Why does Sagen do so at this point in the process? Is it simply to engage Joe further? Is it because he can see how injured and frightened Joe is and he wants to offer some reassurance? Could there be any other reason?

Epilogue

An Extraordinary Leader's Farewell

In his retirement speech, Joe thanks his
teammates and bids them a fond farewell.

An Extraordinary Leader's Farewell

"My friends, as you know, this is my last day to work at KC Miller Conveyor.

"I stand before you a man of advanced age, having worked with you 50 years now. Those years have escorted me through all the chapters of a lifetime. I was an innocent young guy in the beginning, with a pudgy face, a full head of hair, and a ready smile. The creases you see now at the edges of my smile have deepened over the years. The wrinkles on my forehead have been hard-earned from raising my eyebrows at some of your stunts, my moments of surprise, and mostly from questioning myself. You cannot see the crow's-feet at the edges of my eyes, because now my eyes hide behind glass. Please know these eyes have had tears of sorrow and tears of joy for you as we have shared our lives together. At times, they have been reddened from lack of sleep, and today they have a great sense of pride as I look at you one final time. I hope you see in them the wisdom of a lifetime and true compassion for each and every one of you.

"Many who retire say they will enjoy relief from the daily grind, pressures, and worries of coming to work. I have no such feelings. Of course, I will enjoy more time with my wife, children, and grandchildren. They all deserve more of my time than I have given them through these years, but I have never resisted or resented the worries and pressures of my work. Rather, I have enjoyed it all and I have looked forward to being here with you every single day.

"There are two powerful reasons I have treasured my time here. The first is a thing we created so long ago, called The KC Miller Way.

We have lived it by always maintaining absolute honesty and integrity in a society that now seems to need that integrity more than ever. And we have lived The KC Miller Way by pursuing our purpose of trying to bring a good life to one another in all we do.

"The second treasure I have found in my time here is you; every single one of you and all the amazing people who have gone before. I am profoundly grateful for having had you and them in my life. Although I am the CEO, the truth is, I look up to you. I admire you as great people who care for each other, are so extremely competent, and have become such a tremendous team.

"What we have created here is remarkable. It goes way beyond just being a well-respected enterprise. It goes beyond our faultless reputation. It even goes beyond our willingness to work through the night to solve a customer's problem. What we have created is a culture in which we have been good to each other, our suppliers, our customers, and the communities in which we work and live.

"I have worked my entire career to become an extraordinary leader. I am not sure I have crossed that finish line, because if I were to come back to work tomorrow, I believe I could find some leadership skill that I should strengthen. Please know, I did this work for you.

"Thank you for your dedication and service. I wish for you all of God's blessings, my friends."

As he speaks, every eye in the room wells up. Some are crying. There is silence. In the back of the room a man stands up. "Good afternoon, Joe. My name is Manny Carrera..."

References

1. Of course, Sagen Cruz is a fictional character and this part of the story deserves further explanation. Ken Olsen at Digital Equipment Corporation is widely credited with giving birth to Matrix Management in the 1980s. The use of cross functional teams dates back to the 1950s.

2. Tirrell, R. (2009). *The Wisdom of Resilience Builders*. Bloomington, IN: Author House.

3. Heifetz, Grashow, and Linsky call this concept "Getting on the Balcony". See note 4, below.

4. Heifetz, R., Grashow, A., Linsky, M. (2009). *The Practice of Adaptive Leadership: Tools and tactics for changing your organization and the world*. Boston, MA: Harvard Business Press.

5. Chrislip, D. D., (2002). *The Collaborative Leadership Fieldbook: A Guide for Citizens and Civic Leaders*. San Francisco. Jossey-Bass.

6. Pearce, C. L., Manz, C., Sims, H. (2009). Where do we go from here? Is shared leadership the key to team success? *Organizational Dynamics*, 38 (3): 234-38.

7. Kanter, R. M. (July-August 1994). Collaborative Advantage: The Art of Alliances. *Harvard Business Review*, HBR online.

8. Ibarra, H. (2015). *Act Like a Leader, Think Like a Leader*. Boston: Harvard Business Review Press.

9. Cameron, E., and Green, M. (2019). *Making Sense of Change Management: A Complete Guide to the Models, Tools, and Techniques of Organizational Change*. New York: Kogan Page, Limited.

10. Burns, J. M. (1978). *Leadership*. New York: Harper and Row.

11. Maslow, A. H. (1954). *Motivation and Personality.* New York. Harper and Row Publishers.

12. The man referenced here is Irv Robinson, retired CEO, Robbie Flexible Packaging Corporation, Lenexa, KS. That company is now TC Robbie, a business unit of TC Corporation.

13. Lencioni, P. (2012). *The Advantage.* San Francisco: Jossey-Bass.

14. Okes, Duke (2019). *Root Cause Analysis: The core of problem solving and corrective action,* Second Edition, Milwaukee, WI, American Society for Quality, Quality Press.

15. Collins, J. C. and Porras, J. I. (1994). *Built to Last.* New York. Harper Business.

16. Ready, D., and Truelove, E. (December 2011). The Power of Collective Ambition. *Harvard Business Review,* HBR online.

17. Bardwick, J. (1991). *Danger in the Comfort Zone.* New York. AMACOM.

18. Leonard, E. C. and Trusey, K. A. (2016). *Supervision: Concepts and Practices of Management.* 13th Edition. Farmington Hills, MI. Cenage Learning.

19. McChesney, C., Covey, S, and Huling, J. (2012) *The Four Disciplines of Execution.* New York. Simon and Schuster.

20. Chris McChesney provides an excellent YouTube overview of the Four Disciplines in action: https://www.youtube.com/watch?v=aEJDliThj7g&t=20s

21. Stack, J. (1992). *The Great Game of Business.* New York. Crown Business.

22. YouTube talk with Jack Stack. https://www.youtube.com/watch?v=S0qw_GX8I5A

23. Hams, B. (2012). *Ownership Thinking.* New York. McGraw-Hill.

A Note to the Discussion Facilitator

Of course, this book can be used for self-study or as a mentor's handbook which can be done by an individual reading this book alone. However, if you intend to use the book as a seminar guide, what follows are some suggestions regarding how to engage your participants in connecting to other books and resources. Rather than have every mentee or seminar member read every book and article, you might wish to assign segments of these resources to various participants who can report their learning to the group and foster interactive discussions. The resources I point to are some of my favorites, but you may have your own favorites as well.

I recommend you seek volunteers to report on any of the following:

Chapters 2 and 4 of *The Wisdom of Resilience Builders* by Rick Tirrell, which discuss competitive platforms. This is about knowing what you are.

Chapters 2 and 6 of *The Wisdom of Resilience Builders* by Rick Tirrell, which discuss the Developmental Frame. This addresses the leadership challenges in the various stages of organizational development.

Chapters 2 and 5 of *The Practice of Adaptive Leadership* by Heifetz, Grashow, & Linsky, regarding Technical vs. Adaptive Leadership.

Any summary found on the Internet regarding Collaborative Leadership. There are many.

Leadership by James MacGregor Burns, Pages 18-23, which defines leadership, Transactional Leadership, and Transformational Leadership.

Pages 232-254 and 401-404 of *Leadership* by James MacGregor Burns, which describes the leadership of Mao Zedong.

Any summary found on the Internet regarding Maslow's hierarchy of needs. Consider using Wikipedia.

Chapters 1 and 6 of *Built to Last* by Jim Collins & Jerry Porras regarding resilient companies and cult-like cultures.

The entire book: *The Advantage* by Patrick Lencioni which discusses the elements of a healthy team. (It is a short book.)

The article: The Power of Collective Ambition by Douglas Ready and Emily Truelove.

The entire book: *The Great Game of Business* by Jack Stack. (Once you start reading this book you will not be able to put it down.)

Acknowledgments

I have been asked how I developed Joe Miller's sixteen leadership Rites of Passage. Likewise, I have been asked how I created the masterful mentoring methods used by Sagen Cruz in these pages. The answer to these two questions reveals the breadth of my gratitude because this book has had many authors, foremost among them are those aspiring leaders and mentors who have been kind enough to seek my counsel. I thank the many who have shared with me their strengths and struggles as they worked to develop their own leadership and mentoring skills. They allowed me to participate. They allowed me to observe. They all authored this book. More than that, I am grateful to each of them for being so remarkably transparent as they shared their lives and leadership with me for so many years.

I would like to point out one special group of people who daily contend with real-world leadership challenges. In addition to leading, they mentor others inside their own organizations who look to them for helpful guidance. Early on in my writing process, I shared a rough draft of this manuscript with them and I thank each of these kindly souls for their review, comments, and advice. More than this, I thank them for the treasured friendships we have developed over the years. They are Don Chew, Pepper Stokes, Louie Malaponti, Peter Young, Byron Pendleton, Jamie Frazier, Todd Geiger, Billy Daniels, Allan Bush, and David Gruner.

A large part of this book was critiqued by an unlikely editor, Andrew Jiron. Andrew is bright, insightful, and exceptionally skilled at studying the concepts herein. He has an impressive ability to correct sentence structure, grammar, and punctuation. He asked hard questions about whether a sentence was needed and where the narrative was taking the reader at a particular moment. What is so unlikely about this editor? Without saying too much, I will just say he is quite young to have handled such crucial responsibilities and he handled them remarkably well. Thank you, Andrew.

I offer thanks to my wife, Barbara, with whom I have shared the journey of a lifetime. Ours has been a unique path and a very good one. I say thank you for your patience with me as my work has so engaged me over the years. You have been on a leadership mission of your own, both in your career and in our family. Your influence has positively affected so many and will continue to do so for generations to come. I give thanks to you as well for your careful review of this book.

It seems that I always involve family in my work. So, I sent the manuscript around and asked for the assistance of some people I treasure greatly. I offer my sincere thanks for reading and reviewing this work to Kate Jiron, Sara and Ryan Cross, and Lisa and Brian Cramer. I thank you for being involved, for being willing to listen, and for showing that my work is important to you.

To all of you, I say thank you. I hope you know that I am constantly aware that I have been profoundly blessed by knowing you.

Annotated Glossary

Adaptive Leadership vs. Technical Leadership
In their book, *The Practice of Adaptive Leadership: Tools and tactics for changing your organization and the world*, Heifetz, Grashow, and Linsky do an impressive job of explaining and teaching about these two concepts. I find these concepts to be quite valuable to leadership coaching. In this book I have simplified the terms to say that Adaptive Leadership is required when a team must do something it doesn't know how to do, and Technical Leadership occurs when the team knows how to do it but the task is not easy.

Call the Process
This, in fact, is a psychological term which seeks to look at what is occurring in a group. This would be helpful in order to determine how many people participated in creating a problem. In management science, begin by examining Continual Process Improvement which seeks ongoing feedback in order to improve performance.

Comfortable Being Uncomfortable
This term was used by Irv Robinson, former CEO of Robbie Fantastic Flexibles Corporation. He encouraged his team to take risks as they attempted to do something they weren't sure they could do.

Competitive Platforms
This is a categorization of four ways that companies operate, and is taken from the book, *The Wisdom of Resilience Builders*. Leaders who create companies that avoid or recover from shocks are called Resilience Builders. They build their firms on four possible Competitive Platforms:

Efficient Platform firms build tremendous internal and external efficiencies to reduce waste and lower costs. They pass those savings on to the consumer. Most big-box discount stores and Internet retailers are built on the Efficient Platform.

Creative Platform firms invent and create new products. Inventing and developing products is extremely costly, so these firms take on a lot of risk. Pharmaceutical companies are Creative Platform firms.

Marketing Platform firms advertise, but they do much more than that. They divide their market into segments and attempt to meet the specific needs of those various segments. Brand image is well crafted and extremely important. Car companies are built on the Marketing Platform.

Relationship Platform firms' primary motive is to increase the attachment a customer has with them. They do the customer favors, even if this means they lose money doing so. They get to know their customers well and use that knowledge to do something pleasing for them. Many architecture firms are built on the Relationship Platform.

Degeneration
Companies tend to travel through four predictable stages of development. Of course, there are some complex theories about these stages, but a concise view would say that there are four broad stages: Growth, Steady-State, Degeneration, and Return to Growth.

Developmental Stages
See the notes in Degeneration.

Dissociative Response

A dissociative response occurs when a person develops a sense that he or she is not experiencing reality. Such a person will say he or she feels like he or she is in a movie or on a television show. Things seem unreal. This is often a reaction to severe stress.

Enter the Cone of Uncertainty

The term, Cone of Uncertainty, is not usually used in business language. Most often it is used in science, especially meteorology. Making predictions and decisions gets easier and more accurate as we travel from the broadest area of the cone down to its most narrow. In this book, I use the term to describe the problem-solving process.

Fishbone Diagram

This is only one of many LEAN tools to examine how many people, departments, and functions have contributed to an outcome; usually a problem. In the diagram, the problem is labeled in a box at the right side of a page and a horizontal line is drawn from the box, out toward the left. Other lines are drawn from each possible source to that horizontal line, one for each potential input.

Go Third Person

This is a phrase that encourages the leader to dial down his or her emotional involvement as problems are addressed and to become objective. I have taken this concept from *The Practice of Adaptive Leadership: Tools and tactics for changing your organization and the world,* by Heifetz, Grashow, and Linsky. They call the process, Getting on the Balcony.

Hope Bearing Plan

This is simply a synonym for a turnaround plan.

LEAN Manufacturing Methods

There is a massive literature on LEAN. Stated most simply, LEAN is the science of doing more with less by reducing waste in areas such as motion, time, defects, inventory, processing, overproduction, and transportation. It relies on five focus areas: value, the value stream, flow, pull, and perfection.

Steady-State and Complacency

In the normal developmental stages of a company (as well as other organizations) once the firm reaches a position of predictable recurring orders and revenues, this is called Steady-State. In most ways, this is a desirable place to be. However, if the teammates begin to reduce their worry or fear that they could lose their competitive advantage, they might become complacent, or too comfortable. Complacency usually precedes degeneration.

Transformational Leadership vs. Transactional Leadership

In his 1978 classic book, *Leadership*, James MacGregor Burns describes Transactional Leadership as a simple transaction between the follower and the leader. So, the follower might offer a vote or some work hours for a tangible anticipated benefit. MacGregor Burns contrasts this with Transformational Leadership, which is motivated by a higher purpose and therefore is highly motivational.

The Four Missions and Their Rites of Passage

First Mission: Take the Lead

First Rite of Passage: All In
Second Rite of Passage: Know What You Are, Know Where You Are
Third Rite of Passage: Enter the Cone of Uncertainty
Fourth Rite of Passage: The Space Between Us
Fifth Rite of Passage: Take the Lead

Second Mission: Create Followers

Sixth Rite of Passage: Create Followers
Seventh Rite of Passage: Respond to Followers' Changing Needs
Eighth Rite of Passage: Transformational Leadership
Ninth Rite of Passage: Get Them All to Be All In

Third Mission: Become a Leader of Leaders

Tenth Rite of Passage: Hand It Over
Eleventh Rite of Passage: Become a Leader of Leaders
Twelfth Rite of Passage: Make Them Partners
Thirteenth Rite of Passage: Empower Your Leaders to Build Their Teams

Fourth Mission: Master the Psychology of Leadership

Fourteenth Rite of Passage: Know Why You Are Here
Fifteenth Rite of Passage: Understand Your Own Dynamics
Sixteenth Rite of Passage: Understand the Dynamics of Others

CPSIA information can be obtained
at www.ICGtesting.com
Printed in the USA
JSHW020958180123
36433JS00001B/59